D0934868

ALL THE KING'S MEN

The Search for a Usable Past

TWAYNE'S MASTERWORK STUDIES

Robert Lecker, General Editor

ALL THE KING'S MEN

The Search for a Usable Past

Harold Woodell

TWAYNE PUBLISHERS • NEW YORK
Maxwell Macmillan Canada • Toronto
Maxwell Macmillan International • New York Oxford Singapore Sydney

Twayne's Masterwork Studies No. 112

All the King's Men: The Search for a Usable Past
Harold Woodell

Twayne Publishers   Maxwell Macmillan Canada, Inc.
Macmillan Publishing Company   1200 Eglinton Avenue East
866 Third Avenue   Suite 200
New York, New York 10022   Don Mills, Ontario M3C 3N1

Library of Congress Cataloging-in-Publication Data

Woodell, Harold, 1941–
    All the king's men : the search for a usable past / by Harold Woodell.
    p. cm. — (Twayne's masterwork studies ; no. 112)
    Includes bibliographical references and index.
    ISBN 0–8057–9411–5 — ISBN 0–8057–8580–9 (pbk.)
    1. Warren, Robert Penn, 1905–89. All the king's men. 2. Literature and history—
United States. 3. History in literature. I. Title. II. Series.
PS3545.A748A7975 1993
813'.52—dc20   92–45601
                                                                    CIP
                                                                    AC

The paper used in this publication meets the minimum requirements of American
National Standard for Information Sciences—Permanence of Paper for Printed Library
Materials. ANSI Z3948-1984. ∞™

10 9 8 7 6 5 4 3 2 1 (hc)
10 9 8 7 6 5 4 3 2 1 (pb)

Printed in the United States of America

Contents

Note on the References and Acknowledgments   *vii*

Chronology: Robert Penn Warren's Life and Works   *ix*

LITERARY AND HISTORICAL CONTEXT

  1.   The Background of the Novel   3

  2.   The Importance of the Work   9

  3.   Critical Reception   12

A READING

  4.   The Narrative   25

  5.   The Road Trip   31

  6.   The Early Campaigns and the Great Sleep   39

  7.   Little Jackie and the Two Impeachment Efforts   48

  8.   Jack the Graduate Student and the Cass Mastern Story   55

  9.   The Case of the Upright Judge   69

  10.   Dr. Stanton and the Willie Stark Hospital   74

  11.   Jack's Trip to the West   82

  12.   Jack Burden's Father   89

  13.   The Assassination of Willie Stark   96

  14.   Resolution and a New Beginning   103

Afterword: Jack Burden—From Cynicism to Acceptance   *109*

Contents

Notes and References   115
Selected Bibliography   117
Index   123

Note on the References and Acknowledgments

The text I have used for this study is the Harvest edition issued by Harcourt Brace Jovanovich in 1982. This paperback volume is readily available and well designed for student use. Page references to the novel are enclosed in parentheses in the following pages.

I gratefully acknowledge the support I received from the College of Liberal Arts and the Department of English at Clemson University, support that made it possible for me to work on this study during a sabbatical. I wish to thank the Jean and Alexander Heard Library at Vanderbilt University for permission to print the photograph of Robert Penn Warren that appears in this volume. I would also like to thank my wife, Libby, not only for her proofreading and suggestions but most of all for her encouragement.

Robert Penn Warren (autographed copy), September 13, 1946
Courtesy of Photographic Archives, Vanderbilt University

Chronology: Robert Penn Warren's Life and Works

1905   Robert Penn Warren is born on 24 April in the small town of Guthrie, Kentucky. Parents are Anna Ruth Penn and Robert Franklin Warren. After Robert, they will have two more children, Mary and Thomas.

1906–1910   Black Patch War in Cumberland Valley region of Kentucky rages between tobacco growers and buyers.

1911–1918   Spends memorable summers on remote tobacco farm with grandfather Gabriel Penn, a Confederate soldier who once rode with Nathan Bedford Forrest. Develops a lasting appreciation for nature. Learns taxidermy.

1920   Graduates from Clarksville (Tennessee) High School, 12 miles from Guthrie, with appointment to U.S. Naval Academy. Accidental eye injury from rock thrown by younger brother Thomas puts end to dream of becoming an admiral in the Pacific Fleet.

1921   Enrolls in Vanderbilt University in Nashville, Tennessee, majoring in chemical engineering. English teachers John Crowe Ransom and Donald Davidson and fellow students Allen Tate and Ridley Wills inspire Warren's commitment to literary study. Fear of blindness in both eyes intensifies over the next three years, eventually leading to severe depression.

1923   Tate introduces Warren to the "Fugitives," a stimulating group of students, teachers, and townspeople interested in the arts, especially poetry. Publishes "Crusade," the first of his 24 poems to appear in the *Fugitive*, the group's literary magazine.

1924   Becomes youngest official member of the Fugitives, destined to lead the South in a literary renaissance. Damaged eye replaced

	with a glass one, thereby ending concern over total loss of vision.
1925	Graduates with B.A. in literature (summa cum laude) from Vanderbilt. Begins "chase after scholarships."
1927	Receives M.A. in literature from the University of California at Berkeley; enters Yale University for postgraduate work.
1928–1930	Becomes Rhodes scholar at New College, Oxford. Publishes *John Brown: The Making of a Martyr*. Writes "The Briar Patch," a conservative segregationist essay, for *I'll Take My Stand*, the major statement of principles of modern southern agrarianism. Receives B.Litt. from Oxford.
1928	Huey P. Long, a person who will have an enormous impact on Warren's career, becomes governor of Louisiana (1928–32) and master of a powerful statewide political machine.
1930	Warren marries Emma Cinina Brescia. Becomes assistant professor of English at Southwestern (Presbyterian) College (now Rhodes College) in Memphis, Tennessee.
1931	Returns to alma mater (Vanderbilt) as assistant professor of English. Publishes first work of fiction, "Prime Leaf," in *The American Caravan*.
1932	Long becomes U.S. senator (1932–35).
1934	Takes position of assistant professor of English (associate, 1936) at Louisiana State University at Baton Rouge. Sees Huey Long political machine at close range. Begins lifelong friendship with Cleanth Brooks. Brooks-Warren collaboration in time produces some of the most influential textbooks in American letters.
1935	Publishes *Thirty-six Poems*, first volume of poetry. With Charles W. Pipkin, Albert Erskine, and Cleanth Brooks, founds the *Southern Review*—with funds provided by Huey Long. Huey Long, now a U.S. senator but still the "Kingfish" of Louisiana, assassinated by Dr. Carl Weiss.
1938	Warren publishes *Understanding Poetry* with Cleanth Brooks; the book redirects literary criticism and eventually radically alters the teaching of literature in American education. Becomes a leader of the New Critics.
1939	Publishes first novel, *Night Rider*, a work centering on the Black Patch War and exploring the disintegrative personality of twentieth-century people.

Chronology

1939–1940	Receives Guggenheim Fellowship. Travels to Italy, witnesses Mussolini's regime, and writes *Proud Flesh*, a verse/prose play about Governor Talos, a dictator from a southern state—the forerunner of *All the King's Men*.
1941	Teaches at the University of Iowa as visiting lecturer.
1942	Publishes *Eleven Poems on the Same Theme*. Takes position of professor of English at University of Minnesota.
1943	Almost unnoticed because of the nation's entry into World War II, *At Heaven's Gate* (second novel) focuses on mob psychology and the tragedy of characters suffering from defects in self-knowledge. With Brooks, publishes *Understanding Fiction*, which does for the study of fiction what *Understanding Poetry* did for the study of poetry.
1944	Issues *Selected Poems, 1923–1943* and accepts chair of poetry at Library of Congress.
1946	Publishes *All the King's Men*. Receives a National Book Award and the Pulitzer Prize in fiction. Also publishes "Blackberry Winter," his best-known short story.
1947	Receives Guggenheim Fellowship. Publishes *The Circus in the Attic and Other Stories*, after which he will write no more short fiction, believing it is detrimental to his short poems.
1949	Movie version of *All the King's Men* (screenplay by Robert Rossen) receives three Academy awards: Best Picture, Best Actor, and Best Supporting Actress. With Brooks, issues *Modern Rhetoric*, eventually a standard text in college composition courses throughout the United States.
1950	Leaves University of Minnesota and joins faculty at Yale University as professor of playwriting. Publishes his most ambitious novel, *World Enough and Time*, loosely based on the "Kentucky Tragedy," a true story of seduction, murder, and suicide that was also the impetus for nineteenth-century works by Charles Fenno Hoffman, Edgar Allan Poe, and William Gilmore Simms. Elected to National Institute of Arts and Letters. Assumes post of chancellor with the American Academy of Poets.
1951	Divorces Emma Brescia Warren.
1952	Marries writer Eleanor Clark.
1953	Daughter Rosanna Phelps Warren born (delivered at home by Warren). Publication of verse novel *Brother to Dragons*, about idealist Thomas Jefferson's confrontation with brutality.

1955	Publishes *Band of Angels* (fifth novel), which explores miscegenation and racial stereotyping. Made into movie starring Clark Gable and Sidney Poitier. Birth of son Gabriel Penn Warren.
1956	Leaves Yale and revisits the South. Modifies earlier racial attitude in *Segregation: The Inner Conflict in the South*, suggesting that race divides not only person from person but also the individual from the self. Travels to Italy.
1957	*Promises: Poems 1954–1956*—written while he was living in a castle on an island off the coast of Italy—acclaimed with National Book Award, Edna St. Vincent Millay Prize, and his second Pulitzer Prize.
1959	Originally titled *The Man Below* and based on an actual event, *The Cave* (sixth novel) is a symbolic study of the subterranean lives of characters trapped in their own selves. Accepts membership in the American Academy of Arts and Letters.
1960	Publishes *You, Emperors, and Others: Poems 1957–1960* and reading version of *All the King's Men: A Play*.
1961	Publishes *Wilderness: A Tale of the Civil War* (seventh novel) and *The Legacy of the Civil War*. Both view the war and individual divisiveness as mirrors of each other. To Warren the Civil War is "the great single event of our history." Returns to Yale as professor of English.
1964	Most roundly denounced of all his novels, *Flood: A Romance of Our Time,* is published.
1965	*Who Speaks for the Negro?* continues involvement in racial issues through interviews with black Americans.
1966	Publishes *Selected Poems: New and Old 1923–1966.*
1967	*Selected Poems* wins coveted Bollingen Prize in poetry.
1968	*Incarnations: Poems 1966–1968* makes extensive use of typography to augment the poems' meaning.
1969	Publishes *Audubon: A Vision*, a volume about the painter-ornithologist who "destroyed beauty in order to create beauty and whet his understanding."
1970	Receives National Medal in Literature. *Audubon* wins Van Wyck Brooks Award.
1971	Publishes *Meet Me in the Green Glen* (ninth novel), a tale of love, murder, and suicide.
1972	Selected for Ten Best Teachers Award at Yale.

Chronology

1973   Retires from Yale to Fairfield, Connecticut.

1974   *Or Else—Poem/Poems 1968–1974*, which may be read as one long poem or as groups of short ones, is published.

1977   *A Place to Come To* (tenth and final novel) considers a placeless modern man who disdains his southern home.

1978   *Now and Then: Poems 1976–1978* wins third Pulitzer Prize.

1980   *Being Here: Poetry 1977–1980* is the poet's "shadowy autobiography." Wins Presidential Medal of Freedom—U.S. government's highest award for a civilian. Named America's "Dean of Letters" by *Newsweek*.

1981   *Rumor Verified: Poems 1979–1980* considers the significance of humanity as it faces mortality. Musical *Willie Stark* premieres. Receives a Prize Fellowship from the John D. and Catherine T. MacArthur Foundation.

1983   Verse/prose work, *Chief Joseph of the Nez Perce* (dedicated to fellow poet James Dickey), examines the plight of the estimable Native American.

1985   *New and Selected Poems, 1923–1985*—the poet at age 80.

1986   Chosen America's first Poet Laureate. Finds the appointment amusing but responds to a charge that poetry is only a pretty affectation with "Pretty, hell! It's life; it's a vital experience."

1988   Contemplates mystery of his father's past in *Portrait of a Father*.

1989   Publishes *New and Selected Essays*, a gathering of his most famous literary essays—eight reprints, five collected for the first time. Dies of cancer on 15 September at age 84.

LITERARY AND HISTORICAL CONTEXT

1

The Background of the Novel

All the King's Men relates both literally and symbolically to the events that shook America and the world at large during the 1930s, a period of human misery and political turmoil known as the Great Depression. During this time charismatic leaders—from Huey Long in America to Benito Mussolini in Italy and Adolf Hitler in Germany—answered the anguished cries of a distressed people and created strong political machines that enabled them to become absolute rulers of their subjects. Robert Penn Warren experienced the American version of the totalitarian state while living in Louisiana and observed another variety of a dictatorship while spending a year in Italy on a study grant.

Warren taught English literature at Louisiana State University when Huey Pierce Long was the undisputed "Kingfish" of the Pelican State, first as governor (1928–32) and then as U.S. senator (1932–35).[1] In Louisiana Warren absorbed the factual and mythical stories about Long while he taught Shakespeare's *Julius Caesar* to college students and read Machiavelli's *The Prince*. In 1938 he received a Guggenheim Fellowship that took him to Mussolini's Italy, and it was there that he began a play, *Proud Flesh*, about a man named Willie Talos, a governor who ruled his state with an iron fist. Warren returned to America and in 1943 began the novel, his third, that he would publish in 1946 as *All the King's Men*, with Willie Stark now the powerful governor of an unnamed southern state.

From the mid-1930s until the mid-1940s, Warren was a close student of the events surrounding the rise and fall of the strong political leader of the variety known as the dictator. He began his contemplations with an actual governor-senator in Baton Rouge and augmented them with direct observations of the Fascists in Rome. Over the years, however, he became less interested in the sensational mechanics of dictatorships the more he thought about larger issues, such as the use to which power is put, the relationship between good and evil, and the problem of self-identity in the modern world.

While *All the King's Men* is not finally about the specifics of the Long regime, it would be fair to say that the novel could not have been written in its present form had Warren not lived and worked in Louisiana during the turbulent years that saw Huey Long at the height of his power and at the time when an assassin's bullet ended Long's career as one of the most unusual figures in American politics.

When Warren crossed the state line of Louisiana in September 1934 to assume his teaching duties at LSU, he entered an earthly kingdom under the near-complete domination of one man, Huey Long. Warren could not have found a more non-American, atypical, volatile scene in the country. The LSU campus was a hotbed of political controversy. It was Long's university—he gave the school money, he appointed the college president (who eventually went to prison), and he once suspended the school paper because it dared criticize him. Oddly enough, though, academic freedom flourished in the classroom because Long did not consider teachers a threat to his power. Rather, he was amused by professorial types in much the same way a more recent politician would dismiss them as "pointy-headed liberals."

Huey Long controlled his state more completely than any other American politician had ever done. At times wildly comic with antics that amused his enemies he accumulated power with a zeal that frightened his closest friends. Seen as a demagogue by some and a savior by others, he was as near a dictator as America has yet produced.

Theoretically he served at the will of the citizens, but in reality Long controlled the ballot box. Yet like many another tyrant, he could not control the aberrant behavior of a would-be assassin.

The Long Revolution started in 1928 when Long became governor of a state that was ripe for social and political upheaval. The movement known as Longism was basically a class struggle with roots in nineteenth-century Louisiana history.[2] By the 1920s tensions between the wealthy planter-business people in the Delta and New Orleans and the poor dirt farmers from the pine barrens in the northern section of the state had reached a breaking point. The planter aristocracy had so controlled politics that small farmers and poor laborers throughout the state had been effectively disempowered from antebellum days into the twentieth century.

The potential for conflict between the haves and the have-nots increased as the "government of gentlemen" continued to ignore the needs of the poorer classes in the state. For example, even before the Civil War the government demonstrated its callousness when the elitist legislature passed a bill that funded public schools based on the number of indigent pupils. Sadly, public schools became stigmatized as "pauper schools" to be avoided by rich and poor alike, with the result that poor whites stopped attending schools, the literacy rate tumbling accordingly. Huey Long would eventually capitalize on this sorry state of affairs.

Seeds of discontent continued to grow throughout the twentieth century as the state government became increasingly unresponsive to the public majority. Near the end of the 1920s the times were ripe for a leader with ambition and ability to take advantage of the bitterness that issued from decades of class antagonism. Such a person was Huey Long.

Long came to power as an advocate of lower-class interests—the first Louisiana governor to use successfully the caste struggle that had been brooding over the state's history for 100 years. He won the 1928 gubernatorial election by promising people all over the state the improvements they so desperately needed—more highways, toll-free bridges, free school textbooks, cheap natural gas for New Orleans, and a new tax on Standard Oil Company. Here at last was the champion of the plain people in their struggles against the wealthy planters and industrialists.

At first amused by what they considered nothing more than a passing oddity in Louisiana politics the old-line aristocracy was startled when Long actually began to carry out most of his campaign promises. Soon he was perceived as a threat to the traditional way of life, and in 1929 the legislature initiated impeachment proceedings to remove him from office. Long, however, was not so easily intimidated, and in a series of maneuvers more crafty than legal he quickly stifled the proceedings. After triumphing over his foes he remarked, "I used to try to get things done by saying 'please.' That didn't work and now I am a dynamiter. I dynamite 'em out of my path" (Sindler, 67).

More determined than ever, Long had his way in the arena of Louisiana politics for the next six years. As a benevolent despot, he doled out schools, roads, hospitals, and textbooks throughout the state. One indication of his accomplishments can be seen in the increase of paved roads from about 230 miles to more than 2,800 and in the number of state bridges from 3 to more than 40 between 1928 and 1935.

All the improvements were sorely needed, but the cost to the people of Louisiana was greater than the bargain. As the Long machine devoured the state, corruption became rampant and political freedom was destroyed. Long eventually gained personal control of every appointed position in the state. Fire and police chiefs, schoolteachers, and janitors in public buildings owed their jobs to him. The democratic process was so suborned that district attorneys and supreme court judges served at the whim of Long's attorney general. One of the government's commissions with the ominous title "The State Bureau of Identification" became known as "Huey's Cossacks." Through autocratic means like these, Long gained complete dominance over the entire state government.

In his introduction to the Modern Library edition of *All the King's Men* Warren tells us that while teaching at LSU, he came up with the idea of a verse play about a southern politician-dictator who lost his life at the hand of an assassin. Warren's character was a "man who in many ways was to serve the cause of social betterment, but who was corrupted by power, even by power exercised against corruption."[3] The politician's power was "based on the fact that somehow he could vicariously fulfill some secret needs of the people about him" ("Intro.," v). Set against this ability was his slow but steady discovery of "his own emptiness and his own alienation" ("Intro.," vi).

After the drama version became the novel the character who had stirred Warren's imagination was named Willie Stark. Thus, *All the King's Men* owes its beginnings to Willie Stark, and Willie Stark's origins can be found in the life of a real southern politician, Governor Huey P. Long of Louisiana. Outwardly the fictional portrait of the Boss looks very similar to the personality and career of the Kingfish (the nickname Long chose for himself from the popular "Amos 'n' Andy" radio show). Both Willie and Huey began life in obscurity, rose to political prominence, and died from assassins' bullets. Early in his career Willie sold Fix-It Household Kits door-to-door, while Huey supported himself by selling patent medicines—which were neither patented nor medicinal—and Cottolene, a vegetable shortening. Willie and Huey attended college for brief periods of time and studied law on their own to pass the state bar examinations. Their campaigns, oratory styles, and political programs resemble each other's, and both men used their offices to reward their followers and to control their opponents. In addition, Huey and Willie looked alike. They were both heavyset, a little under six feet tall, and had big brown eyes, thick brown hair, and faces that were becoming a bit jowly. Huey Long was killed on the floor of the Louisiana Capitol by Dr. Carl Weiss, a physician, who shot him with a small-caliber pistol for no clearly discernible reason, although a theory developed that Weiss possibly believed that Long was trying to destroy his family's reputation. Except for the assassin's motive, Willie Stark's death is a near duplicate of his real-life counterpart's.

Was Huey Long a courageous representative of the people who helped them share in the American dream, or was he a petty despot motivated by a lust for power? He did help the poor, but he also subverted the legal process. He gave the people what they needed, but in the end he robbed them of their heritage as free American citizens. Replacing aristocracy with autocracy did not lead to the growth of sane government and responsible public policy. The paradox of Longism—that good can come from bad—lies at the core of *All the King's Men*.

2

The Importance of the Work

All the King's Men is America's most successful political novel and the benchmark against which all other such novels are judged in both craftsmanship and thematic development. At present it is the only American novel that compares favorably with such European works as Conrad's *Nostromo* (1904), Dostoyevski's *The Possessed* (1913), and Koestler's *Darkness at Noon* (1941). Curiously enough, *All the King's Men* retains its preeminence because it exceeds the normal category of the political novel through its insights into eternal human questions about freedom, responsibility, and self-identity. For these reasons it has endured while other American political novels have dwindled in readership as their topical subjects have faded like the headlines in last week's newspapers.

While American authors have written dozens of novels on the general subject of politics, the American landscape has by and large proved barren soil for works about the machinations of politicians and alternate political theories that would test America's political order. The reason is fairly clear—America's success story with its experiment in democracy has made all challenges to the Republic, except for the Civil War, transitory or insignificant. European countries have undergone turmoil that dismantled entire political systems and replaced them with others, but America's ship of state has sailed along for more than 200 years with the twin rudders of the Constitution and the Bill of Rights. By no means perfect, America's system of government continues to weather the storms of change successfully.

A result of a stable political arena is that American writers of fiction in general have explored only in muckraking and journalistic exposés the corruption in American government, or they have revealed the sordidness of public affairs that sensitive people find reprehensible. For example, Harriet Beecher Stowe's *Uncle Tom's Cabin* (1852) is a political novel in the sense that it attempts to correct an institutional evil within the body politic. And Henry Adams's *Democracy* (1880) examines the underhanded practices of lobbyists and the members of Congress during the Grant presidency. Further, Hamlin Garland's *A Spoil of Office* (1892) looks at the ways big business influences government. Rarely does a reader find an American novel like Jack London's *The Iron Heel* (1908) with its acclaim of a fascist oligarchy or Upton Sinclair's *Oil!* (1926), a socialist tract that condemns capitalism.

Only a handful of American political novels has received a wide readership and some lasting acclaim. Among these are Lionel Trilling's *The Middle of the Journey* (1947), John Dos Passos's *The Grand Design* (1949), Edwin O'Connor's *The Last Hurrah* (1956), and Allen Drury's *Advise and Consent* (1959). While at times interesting, these novels are limited in scope or weakened by the topicality of subject matter. By and large, the best of the American political novels have explored the politician as a corruptible human being who through greed or a lust for power manipulates the democratic system but fails in the end because the people and the system are basically healthy and sound.

Four such novels were written about the career of Huey Long: Hamilton Basso's *Sun in Capricorn* (1942), John Dos Passos's *Number One* (1943), Adria Locke Langely's *A Lion Is in the Streets* (1945), and Robert Penn Warren's *All the King's Men* (1946). The first three of these are concerned with fragments of Longism, and each shows the Huey Long character as a dictator. Gilgo Slade, Chuck Crawford, and Hank Martin begin with nothing more than ambition and a talent for swaying the masses, and each becomes a victim of the power he wields over his followers. All are at times engrossing portraits of the American fascist, yet none rises above a stereotype of the dictator.

All the King's Men engages the reader's interest in a way these other novels do not because as a political novel it explores not only the rise of a demagogue but also the relationship between the powerful leader and his followers, an exploration that in turn leads to a consideration of the connection between justice and power, how each is gained, maintained, and lost. Willie Stark never becomes an American version of the Nazi beast. Even when Stark is at his worst, the reader is aware of his potential for good, which is not to say that he is not a dangerous threat to democracy. Cousin Willie is a southern American farmboy who through good intentions gains control of a political machine because he responds to the needs of ordinary people who ask for his help. Once he is in power his motives may change and he does commit immoral acts to achieve his ends, but he is never lost in an all-destroying gluttony of power. Contrary to the reader's expectations, Willie almost comes out all right at the end—as many of America's own flawed political leaders have a way of doing.

Finally, *All the King's Men* is an important novel because of its portrait of the developing sensibilities of a twentieth-century man, the story's narrator, Jack Burden, whose mind filters the saga of Willie Stark and his followers. Jack tells the reader everything he or she needs to know to interpret the tragedy of Willie and in the process lays bare his own soul as it becomes entangled in the Boss's web. Thus, *All the King's Men* is more than a sensational story about a homegrown dictator and his cohorts; rather, it is a complex narrative that weaves together separate strands of narrative involving several themes. By giving the reader a political novel with two developing characters, Jack and Willie, Robert Penn Warren created a modern masterpiece in the art of fiction, one that is assured of its place as an American classic.

3

Critical Reception

When *All the King's Men* was published by Harcourt, Brace and Company on 17 August 1946, it became an immediate best-seller. The first pressrun of 7,500 copies was followed by four more, and by 1949 close to 40,000 copies were in print, including an Armed Services paperback edition. Other editions were soon published, including the Time Magazine Reading Program edition (1963), the Franklin Library edition (1976), and even a "Ladder" edition (1973), a 132-page abridged version with a 3,000-word-level vocabulary. With the 1955 edition, well over 2 million copies were in circulation. The blurb on the cover then read "The world-famous American novel of power and corruption, and the meteoric rise and fall of Willie Stark—politician," indicating the book marketers' desire to capitalize on what had become the standard impression of the novel's content. By now *All the King's Men* has gone through some 50 printings and been translated into 24 foreign languages.

The novel's popularity led Columbia Pictures to purchase the screen rights to *All the King's Men*, and in 1949 the movie came to the screen with a script written by Robert Rossen, who would also write *Lilith* and *The Hustler*. The movie was a great success both popularly and critically, earning an Academy Award, the New York Film Critics Award, and the Golden Globe Award for the best motion picture of the year. In addition, Broderick Crawford, who played Willie, won an Oscar for Best Actor, and Mercedes McCambridge took another one for Best Supporting Actress as Sadie. The movie focused almost entirely on Willie Stark, as illustrated by the title of the movie review in *Life* magazine: *"All the King's Men*: The Prize Novel about a Demagog Makes Year's Most Exciting Movie."

All the King's Men was widely reviewed when it was first published, and the responses were positive for the most part. There were, however, some exceptions, and a few readers were even appalled by the book. The writer for *Catholic World* objected to the moral bankruptcy of the "motley" characters, whose language was "coarse, blasphemous, and revolting" and whose actions, he claimed, would "shame a pagan hottentot."[1] Harold Gardiner in "Why Put Him Together Again?" denounced Willie as a dictator and Jack as an empty man given to "phony theologizing."[2] He thought the novel would be interesting only as an example of "abnormal psychology."

Most of the reviewers who faulted the novel did so on polemical grounds—the book had neither roundly denounced totalitarianism nor portrayed the demagogue as a villainous tyrant from first to last. Some believed Warren had even written a book in praise of the archetypal fascist. An author for the *Christian Science Monitor* declared, "If the late Huey Long is Mr. Warren's prototype, as seems likely, complaint may be made that the author has been too kind to his subject."[3] Orville Prescott's generally admiring piece in the *Yale Review* chided Warren for "his refusal to consider Huey Long as the American variety of fascist he really was, instead of as just a mixture of idealism and corruption."[4] Of all who were offended by the novel, perhaps fellow novelist Hamilton Basso delivered the most damaging assessment in a *Life* essay that rebuked Warren for not completely condemning the Long-like figure as he had done in his own novel, *Sun in Capricorn*. According to Basso, the Long character should be portrayed as evil, proud, and ambitious, not shown with any redeeming qualities as Warren had done. Basso's article marked the beginning of a long and sometimes acrimonious debate between Warren's supporters and detractors about the value of all of Warren's work, a debate that would not subside until the 1960s.

In addition to the objections to the novel for its allegedly kind treatment of a dictator, another flaw to which some readers pointed was the depiction of "the king's men" as "collaborators." In a post–World War II America with the many examples of the armies of occupation fresh in mind, anything that even hinted at collaboration was condemned as evil. For instance, Adam Stanton's support of Willie's hospital project reminded a few readers of the French people who had assisted the Germans during the occupation of their country. Thus, Robert Davis in his article "Dr. Adam Stanton's Dilemma" in the *New York Times Book Review* lamented what he saw as a good man caught up in "the ethics of collaboration."[5]

To some critics, then, Warren had just not written the novel he should have written, and the "Long" note they hit in these early reviews would linger on to influence later evaluations of the novel.

By far, though, the reviewers saw the publication of *All the King's Men* as a landmark in Warren's career and in some cases in twentieth-century American fiction. Diana Trilling in the *Nation* praised it as a "very remarkable piece of novel-writing" and applauded its "largeness of intention." She concluded that "Mr. Warren's study of a political leader is intended to investigate the moral relativism inherent in the historical process."[6] George Mayberry in the *New Republic* compared it favorably with *Moby-Dick, the Adventures of Huckleberry Finn, The Great Gatsby*, and *The Sun Also Rises* and declared that a modern novel that was a good story, a political as well as a philosophical novel, was a rarity. He believed *All the King's Men* was "the finest American novel in more years than one would like to have to remember."[7] J. P. Wood in the *Saturday Review of Literature* proclaimed, "There are not too many good political novels. This is one. More important, it is a good novel, and at any time there are even fewer of them."[8] Granville Hicks in *American Mercury* said that Warren's story about the meaning of history and human life put him in "the very front rank of American novelists."[9]

Henry Rago in *Commonweal* struck the most perceptive chord when he noted that *All the King's Men* "assures Robert Penn Warren of a place among the handful of novelists in America worth taking seriously."[10] Rago was unusual in his insight about the role Jack Burden plays in the novel. For him the novel was not just about Willie Stark but "about the South, about America, and about all men in 'the terrible division' of modern society"—a situation best demonstrated in Jack Burden (Rago, 599). Concerning the assertion by Jack that Willie might have achieved some good, he exclaimed, "it is inexcusable to read this passage as a eulogy to Huey Long" (Rago, 600).

If the initial reception was somewhat mixed, the critical attention *All the King's Men* received grew dramatically over the next few years until the book was universally hailed as one of the great American novels of the twentieth century.

Almost immediately after the publication of *All the King's Men*, literary critics began to take a longer and deeper look at the novel and were impressed by the power and earnestness they found in the work. Two of the first of these examinations were by Robert B. Heilman and Norton R. Girault, who in 1947 wrote what would stand as not only pioneering works on the novel but also as enduring essays well worth reading today. Heilman's "Melpomene as Wallflower; or, the Reading of Tragedy" asserted that *All the King's Men* had restored the classical ideal of tragedy in a contemporary narrative through Jack Burden, the modern person in search of self-knowledge. Girault's "The Narrator's Mind as Symbol: An Analysis of *All the King's Men*" insisted on the centrality of Jack Burden to the narrative and stressed the idea of his rebirth as the unifying theme of the novel.

Despite this early promising turn to Jack Burden as the center of the novel, a few writers continued to pursue the Huey Long connection that had captured the interest of the first reviewers. Essays by Oscar Cargill ("Anatomist of Monsters"), Orville Prescott ("The Political Novel: Warren, Orwell, Koestler"), and W. M. Frohock ("Mr. Warren's Albatross") examined more fully than the reviewers had done the political and philosophical ramifications of the portrait of an American demagogue as seen in Willie Stark. The most useful study on the relationship between the real-life strongman and the fictional character is Ladell Payne's "Willie Stark and Huey Long: Atmosphere, Myth, or Suggestion?" Payne's essay describes convincingly that many of the external elements in the fictional portrait of Willie Stark rely heavily on both the career and the personality of Huey Long—despite Robert Penn Warren's denial to the contrary.

Following the promising beginning indicated by the Heilman and Girault essays in 1947, dozens of excellent studies have been published on *All the King's Men*; taken together, they span the whole range of modern literary study, from traditional historical criticism through formalism to radical deconstructionism. Studies of the work show a variety of interests and a diversity of approaches unique in the examination of a single modern novel. Theologians, journalists, political scientists, and historians, in addition to literary scholars, have been fascinated by various elements in the text. For example, the titles alone of a few of the more outstanding essays indicate how stimulating the novel has been to various critics: "Robert Penn Warren's Novels: The Symbolic and Textual Patterns," by John M. Bradbury; "Polarity of Themes in *All the King's Men*," by Elizabeth Kerr; "Robert Penn Warren and the Confessional Novel," by Neil Nakadate; "Robert Penn Warren's *All the King's Men*: A Novel of Pure Imagination," by Christopher G. Katope; and "Burden's Complaint: The Disintegrated Personality as Theme and Style in Robert Penn Warren's *All the King's Men*," by Jerome Meckier. These essays also indicate the progressive move away from politics to the universal problems of the narrator as the focus of the novel.

Further evidence of the growing importance of *All the King's Men* in American fiction is found in the presence of several collections of critical essays devoted solely to the work. The first of these was a five-essay collection published in *Folio* in 1950 and titled *"All the King's Men": A Symposium."* In 1957 the Carnegie Institute of Technology published seven essays with the same title, *"All the King's Men": A Symposium.* Maurice Beebe and Leslie A. Field edited a compilation of 25 selections as *"All the King's Men": A Critical Handbook (1966).* James F. Light edited the 14-essay volume *The Merrill Studies in "All the King's Men" (1971),* and Robert H. Chambers brought together 11 essays in 1977 as *Twentieth Century Interpretations of "All the King's Men."* These five collections assemble many of the finest essays on the novel with very little duplication, *a*nd several of them contain original pieces written for the compilation. Contemporary students interested in researching the novel should take advantage of these convenient anthologies, each of which has made an important contribution to the novel's growing reputation.

In addition to the many essays on his novel by a host of critics, Robert Penn Warren has provided ample commentary of his own about the origins and interpretations of *All the King's Men.* Beginning in 1947 with a one-page article in the *Chicago Sunday Tribune Magazine of Books,* he explains that the novel began as a play that became too complex and so he turned to the novel, which he wrote between 1943 and 1945. In 1953 Warren wrote an essay for the *Sewanee Review* that was used as the introduction to the Modern Library edition of the novel. In it he revealed that Jack Burden's role grew from minor to major, and that, regarding the use of Huey Long, "suggestion does not mean identity."11 In other words, Long had simply started him thinking about the role of the powerful leader in a democracy. In the Yale Review in 1964 Warren published *"All the King's Men: The Matrix of Experience,"* which dwelt at length on the Long–Stark connection and the fascinating variety of life the author had discovered while he was teaching in Louisiana. And in several interviews, the most notable one appearing in the *Paris Review* and conducted by Ralph Ellison and Eugene Walter, Warren discusses the parallels between *All the King's Men* and his other novels, the significance of Jack Burden, and various technical problems in the craft of fiction.

The critical attention devoted to *All the King's Men* over the nearly five decades since its publication is a good mirror of the evolution present-day readers may experience as they explore the novel for the first time. The history of the critical reception shows a movement from the political relevancy of the novel with an interest in the biography of Huey Long to the examination of Willie Stark as a man of power and finally to the role of the narrator, Jack Burden, as the central character of the work. That any one novel would inspire such a wide array of opinions and commentary is a testimony to the rich complexity of the text and a tribute to Warren's craftsmanship as a master of the modern novel form.

One final note. In the May 1990 issue of *Southern Living* the editors published the results of a poll they had conducted among "Southern novelists, poets, story writers, journalists, critics, and scholars" to determine the top 10 favorite works in southern literature. In a list of books dominated by William Faulkner and containing volumes by Eudora Welty, Flannery O'Connor, and Walker Percy the second work in the list headed by *Absalom, Absalom!* is Robert Penn Warren's *All the King's Men*—another indication of the novel's continuing holding power among the literary experts of the American South.

A READING

Accepting the Past

How does one generation learn to accept the strengths and reject the weaknesses of the past? An answer to this question involves the timeless issues of freedom and responsibility—subjects addressed throughout *All the King's Men* in theme, structure, and characterization. According to Warren, in order for individuals to achieve a reasonable portion of independence they must free themselves from the past's cultural limitations and at the same time hold fast to the nurturing qualities that are worth passing down from one generation to the next. Freedom comes from learning to recognize and deal with those elements in a society which limit growth and understanding. Responsibility is the acceptance of a person's connections with the past and an acknowledgment of the person's duty to those with whom he or she shares a common heritage and humanity. Both aspects—living freely and accepting responsibility—require learning to respect oneself and one's neighbors despite the blindness, hypocrisy, indifference, and pride that often mar human relationships.

This complex issue of learning how to live in the present while accepting the past lies at the heart of much of the literature written during the southern literary renaissance (1920–50). Variations on the conflict between the past and the present are found in the works of such writers as William Faulkner, Allen Tate, Katherine Anne Porter, and Thomas Wolfe. In Faulkner's *The Sound and the Fury*, for instance, Quentin Compson goes to a watery suicide because he cannot stop time and prevent his sister, Caddy, from discrediting the family's ancient honor through her promiscuity. In the poem "Ode to the

Confederate Dead" Tate's modern southerner stands outside the cemetery gates, unable to penetrate the mystery of time in a failed attempt to make contact with a meaningful past. In "The Jilting of Granny Weatherall" Porter's Granny Weatherall slips into her eternal sleep while suffering from long-ago emotional wounds. And in Wolfe's *Look Homeward, Angel* Eugene Gant desperately seeks to flee his dysfunctional mountain family, while carrying with him into the big cities of the North a destructive heritage of alcoholism.

In all four of these works characters suffer or cause others to suffer because they are unable to forgive past hurts resulting from misunderstanding and misapplication of southern cultural traditions. Quentin wants Caddy to play the role of the southern belle; Tate's unnamed southerner believes his own life is narrow and hopeless when judged against the nobility of Confederate warriors; Granny feels betrayed by a man and Christ; and Eugene is crippled by the demands of his patriarchal family. Quentin, Tate's southerner, Granny, and Eugene all fail, in one way or another, to adjust to the spiritual and psychological pressures brought to bear on the modern southerner as the old generation is replaced by the new. Thus it is with *All the King's Men,* and while the basic conflict of the novel resembles that of many another novel and poem from the southern literary renaissance, Warren's solution to the twin problems of achieving freedom and accepting responsibility reveals an original talent fascinated with a new exploration of the frontiers of what it means to be a modern southerner in the New South.

In *All the King's Men* the universal conflict between the past and the present develops as a specific struggle between the cultures of the Old South and the New South. Although a strict historical interpretation defines the Old South as existing from 1820 to the Civil War, in the geographic region known as the Deep South—the setting of Warren's novel—the cultural patterns of the Old South remained powerful through the 1920s—the time of *All the King's Men.* In the novel traditional southern beliefs are pitted against modern values in such a dynamic way that the novel at times resembles more a clash between different nations than a single culture at war with itself. Throughout the novel, Judge Irwin and his circle represent the standards of the Old

South and Willie Stark and his assistants stand for the values of the New. The battleground over which the combat rages lies within the personality of Jack Burden—a modern southerner caught between the opposing worldviews. Jack's burden is to reconcile the best of the two worlds.

THE SIGNIFICANCE OF NAMES IN THE NOVEL

In the real world the names people are born with indicate nothing at all about their personalities. Even nicknames that point out an obvious bodily feature, such as "Shorty" or "Fatso," do not reveal what a person is like on the inside. Unless a person belongs to the criminal underworld, he or she is unlikely to be tagged with a name like "Snake" or "Killer," names that may announce a major personality trait but here again assigned to people after they are born. In literature, however, names of characters are often significant and help to provide the reader with an interpretation of the character's true self. Thus, in Nathaniel Hawthorne's *The Scarlet Letter* the names Chillingworth and Dimmesdale are signals to the reader that one of these men is coldhearted and the other is having difficulty finding his way. The main character in Henry James's *The American* is named Christopher Newman, a name suggesting both the discoverer of America and the hero's innocence.

In *All the King's Men* Robert Penn Warren also uses names as an aid to characterization. Names like Burden and Stark alert the reader to the hardship that one character endures and the severity of the other. In this respect the names in the novel are connotative in the same way those by Hawthorne and James are. Warren, however, uses the characters' names in another way as well—to remind the reader of the duality of human experience. Except for the stereotyped roles of the minor characters, most of the characters are neither all good nor all bad but instead a complex mixture of the saint and the sinner—in other words, realistic characters who think and act like actual human beings. Warren emphasizes this fact of human nature through the use of contrasting first and last names. If a reader considers only the first names of the characters—Jack, Willie, Lucy, Tiny, Sadie, Gummy, Anne, and Adam—he or she is likely to think of the novel as a redneck version of the pastoral, with good old boys and girls engaging in pleasant, harmless activities. To isolate the characters by last name alone would exaggerate the bleak side of human nature. Burden, Stark, Stanton, Larson, and Mastern are names that sound ominous and suggest grim conclusions. By considering the combination of the first and last names—Willie and Stark, for example—the reader may gain an insight into the true identity of the characters in a novel that to a great extent is about the search for self-identity.

4

The Narrative

Tell me a story of deep delight.

—Audubon: A Vision

Robert Penn Warren was first and foremost a storyteller. Whether in a novel like *All the King's Men*, a poem like "The Ballad of Billie Potts," a short story like "Blackberry Winter," or even a critical essay on Coleridge's "The Rime of the Ancient Mariner," Warren loved to tell a story that would engage the reader and lead him or her into the magical realm of the imagination. His dedication to the power of narration was centered on his desire to learn about humankind's self-identity in its fall through time. These were the two constants in his career, the twin wellsprings of all his art: the quest for self and storytelling.

All the King's Men, the third of 10 novels Warren wrote in his lifetime, is notable for its distinctive narrative form. It does not resemble any of the other 9 novels in the way it is put together, but neither do any two Warren novels resemble each other. Warren, like that other master storyteller from the South, William Faulkner, believed that every good story he told should be different from all the other ones that had come before. Both Warren and Faulkner adhered to the original meaning of the word *novel* as "something new, unusual, or different" as it applied to the prose narrative. Thus, Faulkner's *The Sound and the Fury* and *Absalom, Absalom!* are so unlike each other in form that they appear to have been written by two different people. So it is with Warren's novels. The person who unravels the plot of *All the King's Men* and decides to read another Warren novel, such as *World Enough and Time* or *The Cave*, will discover a similar phenomenon—a master craftsman who refused to duplicate past efforts. Warren once said in an interview, "I have a horror of self-imitation. I don't want to repeat myself."[1] No other author has been more perceptive in evaluating the writer's own motivation for composition. Had he wanted to, Warren could have turned out popular historical novels like sweet rolls, but to have done so would to him have been the artistic equivalent of the Unpardonable Sin.

All the King's Men is a rarity in modern fiction—a complex narrative that challenges the reader but finally resolves itself and rewards the reader with a solid sense that he or she has been in the company of a great storyteller. If at times the reader is puzzled, he or she might recall that millions of people have read this novel, unriddled its plot complications, and declared it a "story of deep delight."

Technically *All the King's Men* is a first-person, retrospective narrative that contains an inset story. What this means is that someone in the narrative speaks directly to the reader about events that have already happened and at some point interrupts the main story to tell an entirely different, self-contained episode. Specifically, Jack Burden, the narrator, tells the reader about people and events in his life that changed his outlook from one of indifference to that of a caring person who is capable of believing that life has some meaning. Along the way the reader learns about the lives of other characters—Willie Stark, Anne and Adam Stanton, Judge Irwin, and Mrs. Burden—as they influence Jack in powerful ways that he does not fully understand until the end of the novel. In other words, Jack writes about his experiences as though they were happening for the first time. At the same time he frequently tells the reader that the way he understood the events in the past is not the way he understands them now in the present. Jack's story is also, then, an autobiography with an underlying element of suspense.

The inset narrative, the self-contained story that interrupts Jack's account of the events surrounding his life, appears in chapter 4 of the novel. Here Jack introduces portions of his great-uncle's journals and letters that he had been editing for his doctoral dissertation until he dropped out of graduate school, despairing of seeing any significance to his work. Called "The Cass Mastern Story," the narrative contained in these papers ostensibly has little or nothing to do with the basic story line, mainly because Jack is unable or unwilling to draw any conclusions about its meaning. Further, the Mastern episode concerns events that transpired during the Civil War era, 50 years before Jack was born. But as the reader learns before Jack does, Cass Mastern's diary, like Jack's own story, is an autobiography of a human being who came to terms with life after great suffering. Only at the end of the novel, after his own immense suffering, will Jack be able to make sense out of "The Cass Mastern Story," to be able to see in it parallels with his own life, and to realize its value as a historical document.

A reader approaching *All the King's Men* for the first time can become momentarily confused by the flow of events that range back and forth over a near-100-year span of southern history, from the antebellum times of Cass Mastern in the 1850s to the post–Willie Stark regime in the late 1930s. The novel, in other words, is not told in a normal time order. It begins in the present near the end of the narrative and moves backward through flashbacks while at the same time moving forward in time to the climax and denouement.

Warren chose to fracture normal chronological time in *All the King's Men* to underscore one of the novel's basic themes: Events in the present are the result of past actions, and they have a direct bearing on future happenings. Thus, a narrative structure that erases the traditional barriers between past, present, and future can help emphasize the interconnectedness of human events. Jack Burden, like Cass Mastern, comes to learn that "the world is all of one piece," resembling a giant spiderweb—and this realization marks his entry into an emotionally mature adulthood (188).

One of the quickest ways of understanding the narrative is to see a brief overview of the major events of the novel arranged in normal time order. The following chronology of the main action will help resolve some of the puzzling plot twists, although it may also take away some of the enjoyment of discovery for readers who like to figure out events on their own. The outline will, however, serve as a road map should the reader become lost somewhere in the network of highways and byways that make up the novel's infrastructure.

The events of the novel fall almost precisely into three segments: (a) the Cass Mastern story, (b) Jack Burden's early life and Judge Irwin's career, and (c) the rise and fall of Willie Stark. All three of these apparently separate narrative units will eventually prove to be intimately connected to one another, through plot parallels, thematic concerns, or cause-and-effect relationships.

The Cass Mastern Story

late 1840s	Cass Mastern and his sister Lavinia (Jack's putative maternal grandmother) are taken in by their older, well-to-do brother Gilbert.
1851	Cass attends Transylvania College in Kentucky.
1852	Cass begins an affair with Annabelle, wife of his friend Duncan Trice.
1854	Duncan commits suicide and Cass leaves Annabelle.
1856	Cass sets his slaves free and attempts to manage his plantation with hired help.
1861	Cass joins the Confederate army when the Civil War breaks out.
1864	Cass, who never fired his weapon in combat, dies in an Atlanta hospital from a war wound.

Jack Burden's Early Life and Judge Irwin's Career

1896	Ellis Burden, a lawyer, marries a young woman from Arkansas.
1897	Jack is born, but it is Judge Irwin, not Ellis Burden, who is his biological father.
1903	On discovery of the affair between Jack's mother and Judge Irwin, Ellis Burden deserts the family.

The Narrative

1910–1915	Jack leads an idyllic childhood with his close friends Anne and Adam Stanton.
1914	Heavily in debt and near bankruptcy, Judge Irwin marries, accepts a bribe, and pays off his debts.
1915	Jack enters college.
1918	Jack and Anne fall in love, but Anne eventually rejects him.
1920	Jack begins graduate study, marries Lois Seager, and becomes a reporter. The marriage lasts about a year.

The Rise and Fall of Willie Stark

1922	Jack meets Willie Stark.
1924	The scandalous collapse of a schoolhouse fire escape prompts Willie into entering politics as a champion of the little people.
1930	Having lost in his first gubernatorial bid four years earlier, Willie is now elected governor of a southern state, presumably Louisiana. Jack begins working for Willie as his special investigative reporter.
1934	After successfully avoiding impeachment the year before, Willie is again elected governor.
1936	On orders from Willie, Jack reluctantly begins to dig into Judge Irwin's past for information to be used against the judge, now one of Willie's political enemies.
1937	Many sensational events occur this year: Judge Irwin commits suicide, Willie begins an affair with Anne, Willie's son Tom crushes his spinal cord in a football game, and Dr. Adam Stanton assassinates Governor Willie Stark.
1938	Willie's son Tom dies. Anne and Jack marry and move into Judge Irwin's house at Burden's Landing.
1939	An older but wiser Jack tells the story of the preceding events and resolves to reenter the world as a concerned citizen.

An examination of the narrative structure and events in each of the 10 chapters of *All the King's Men* reveals just how skillful Warren was in crafting a novel composed of seemingly disparate elements that finally come together in a unified whole. Here again, as in the fracturing of the normal chronology, Warren makes the novel's structure support a major thematic concern: Out of chaos can come order, even if it is tentative and momentary. Apparently random events in the life of

Jack Burden do eventually fit together like the pieces in a jigsaw puzzle, and when all of the events fall into place they will do so because Jack wanted to understand them. Jack will then have become a free, responsible person, aware of the possibility of harmony in the world despite its inevitable suffering and uncertainty.

5

The Road Trip

All the King's Men begins with a chapter that dramatically yokes the opposing cultures of the Old and the New South through the structural device of an automobile trip composed of four segments. The first takes place in a Cadillac speeding along Highway 58, the second in Mason City, the next on Willie Stark's homesite, and the last at Judge Irwin's house. This road trip is one of several that will appear in the novel as a recurring motif.

The four units of the road trip move from the modern New South of powerful automobiles and efficient highways, to an example of the modern politician in action, to an old farm of the plain folk, and finally to a representative mansion and gentleman of the Old South. With its segments equally balanced between the modern and the traditional, the journey is in effect one of a return through time from the New to the Old. The trip begins with one of the most frequently used symbols of the modern world—the automobile—and ends with images that represent the two layers of the culture of the Old South—the farmhouse of the hardworking poor whites and a mansion reminiscent of an antebellum manor house.

HIGHWAY 58

Jack Burden begins in medias res, that is, in the midst of things, and grabs the reader's attention immediately with an account of an automobile speeding through a southern countryside. While historians and sociologists speak of the "bulldozer" revolution that brought the South into the twentieth century, poets and novelists are more prone to use the automobile as a symbol of the South's modernity. Not only is it a machine capable of great destruction, but it also can move its passengers away from the land, a traditional source of sustenance, and away from the cares and considerations that arise from normal human contact. From William Faulkner to Flannery O'Connor, writers of the southern literary renaissance see the automobile as a disruptive force in the southern landscape. (Hazel Motes in O'Connor's *Wiseblood* exclaims ironically, "A man with a good car don't need Jesus!"). Warren too uses the motorcar to stand for southern progress, but he does not completely reject it as other writers have done. While clearly admiring the smooth lines and powerful engine of a sleek machine, Warren more typically focuses on the cars' drivers. If their motivations are selfish, then the car may turn into a weapon. On the other hand, the automobile may console a driver like Jack Burden, who is looking for a purpose in life.

The time is 1936, and the place is Highway 58, a new concrete road that runs from the capital (unnamed but apparently Baton Rouge, Louisiana) to Mason City, a town near Governor Willie Stark's birthplace. The scene opens with Jack Burden, Willie Stark, Lucy (Willie's wife), Tom (his son), and Tiny Duffy (a flunky) in a Cadillac chauffeured by Sugar-Boy O'Sheean, a half-crazed speed demon and gunman devoted to Willie. The trip down this straight white modern highway—a product of Willie's term in office—is harrowing because of the great speed at which they are traveling and the constant potential for disaster. At any moment the car could hook a wheel on the shoulder and the passengers could be destroyed in the blink of an eye.

In addition to focusing the reader's attention, the automobile ride allows Jack to acquaint the reader with the changing landscape as they travel from south to north through a state under the nearly complete domination of the Boss, Willie Stark. From the cottonfields of the flat lowlands to the small farms that dot the red-clay hill country, it is a blighted land, peopled with poor whites and even poorer blacks living on the borderline of poverty—it is just such a land and people that made possible the rise of a demagogue/politician like Willie Stark.

This automobile trip through Mason City and on to other places occurs in only a few hours during one hot summer afternoon and night but covers several hundred miles of highway. Traveling at a frantic pace, the modern luxury car races from place to place at the command of Willie Stark. The car and the trip illustrate both his powerful personality and his ability to make quick decisions that commit him and his followers to purposeful action.

Even though Sugar-Boy is the skillful driver of the powerful car, Jack's narration shows that the real force driving the swift events in this chapter is Willie Stark. Without Willie there would be no splendid new highway traversing the boondocks, no elegant luxury car, and no Jack Burden to live in the Boss's reflected light. Willie Stark is the New South's politician—blessed with intelligence, full of energy, and sure of purpose. But like the onrushing limousine, Willie too possesses a latent potential for destructive action, a capacity to obliterate anything that stands in his way—even his own best self and his closest companions as well.

Mason City

Willie's Cadillac, followed by another car filled with reporters, stops at Mason City. Along with his entourage, Willie enters the town's drugstore, where he is greeted with reverence and enthusiasm by the customers. After showing concern for an old-timer's problem, Willie strolls calmly out to the town square, where he delivers a mesmerizing speech. Willie, a man of the people, knows well how to charm and manipulate his listeners.

During this episode Willie is in complete control, confident of his power to touch these plain folk through a spontaneous speech that flows naturally, one filled with folksy metaphors, rural anecdotes, and biblical allusions. And although it appears to be just a friendly talk to his neighbors, Willie's address cleverly affirms that he is the only politician in the state that these poor people can trust. Politicians from the old government have ignored them, but Willie will always be their champion. By giving them hope that he alone will alleviate their poverty and suffering, Willie breaks sharply from the politicians of the old order, those interested only in lining their own pockets. In Willie's New South the poor and the powerless will no longer have to endure the empty promises and indifference of the old style politicos.

Willie and his people then leave Mason City, and as they pass an old schoolhouse on the edge of town Jack glimpses an image that reminds him of his first meeting with Willie some 14 years earlier. The extended memory that follows is the first of many flashbacks that occur throughout the narrative.

A reporter for the big-city newspaper, the *Chronicle*, Jack Burden had first met the Boss when Willie, the county treasurer of Mason County, had come to the capital on business relating to a school-bond issue. During this reminiscence Jack interposes two more memories of subsequent events, ones occurring during Willie's governorship, that had their seeds in this fateful meeting. Jack's memories in this flashback show the reader just how far Willie has come from the teetotaling bumpkin wearing a Christmas tie in Slade's pool hall to the powerful governor who now drinks his liquor with ease while delivering cynical remarks about his closest political allies.

When Willie first entered politics in Mason City, he was elected county treasurer. From all appearances, he believed he could make a difference through honesty and hard work. He came from a poor but dignified farm family and had married a local schoolteacher, a good woman named Lucy. Working diligently to improve his life throughout his early manhood, Willie resembles Abraham Lincoln with his single-minded devotion to study and self-improvement. Willie's early life is a southern agrarian version of the American myth of the self-made person.

The earliest glimpse the reader has of Willie is of a rustic wearing a cheap seersucker suit, high-topped black shoes, a shirt with a high collar, and a mismatched tie. Everything about his appearance is plain and straightforward. He has no pretentious mannerisms and shakes hands with strangers forthrightly. He looks and acts more like a Sunday-school teacher than a southern politician—a point illustrated in the contrast between him and the arrogant Tiny Duffy with his shiny gold tooth. At this point in his career Willie is a good man who wants to serve the people the best he can.

Willie's journey to power has been long and difficult, one the reader will learn about later in more detail. Nevertheless, it is clear that Willie has been amazingly successful in his climb over the good-old-boy politicians of his state and that his success is genuinely admired by Jack Burden, Willie's chief "research assistant" and narrator of these events. It is also worth noting that whatever Willie was when he first began his quest for power, he is no longer that entity. The Willie Stark of the present is still a man of good intentions, but he has become cynical about the people he once admired. The reader senses that this powerful, charismatic leader may do a great deal of harm should he ever decide to do so.

OLD MAN STARK'S FARM

Warren's version of the Old South in this novel is composed of two parts: the white plain people and the aristocrats. (An important third segment of the traditional South, the black population, only rarely appears in this work.) The plain people and the aristocrats share many values; they both believe in the family, the land, hard work, and honor. Southern aristocrats nurture their family lineages more carefully and place a greater emphasis on class structure than the plain people do. A significant political difference between the two is that while they are both conservative, the plain folk are potentially more receptive to change—especially if a new political program calls for higher taxes on the gentry or some other redistribution of the wealth, as Willie's does.

Two automobiles, Willie's and the reporter's, turn from the highway onto the dirt road leading to a farm out in the country where Old Man Stark still lives in an unpainted wooden house, unimpressive but still better than most throughout a region of scrub pines and washed-out gullies. The reason for Willie's road trip with his wife and son now becomes clear. He wants to provide the reporters with a photo opportunity in a rustic setting with the Old Man, the results of which will reaffirm his ties to his place of origins among the plain people, the source of his political strength.

After Willie and Mr. Stark greet each other in a somewhat formal manner, Jack turns his attention briefly to Willie's wife, Lucy, and imagines what it must have been like when Willie and Lucy were first married. In Jack's fanciful creation, which the reader accepts as thoroughly plausible, Willie studied law books upstairs in the farmhouse while Lucy and Mr. Stark sat quietly before a peaceful fireplace. This vision of family contentment will prove ironic when the reader discovers the actual status of Willie and Lucy's marriage at this time in their lives. A short time later Jack makes a similar imaginative leap even further back in time, to when Willie was a schoolboy studying by coal oil in that same cold, austere room and becoming aware for the first time of the mysterious stirrings of his latent ambition. While the reader never fully understands the subtle mixture of heredity and environment that made Willie the unique person he is, he or she can begin to see that Willie's plain-folk heritage has contributed much to the person he is now. Hard work, a stubborn willingness to pursue a goal, but above all a belief that he is important enough to make a difference despite the odds are all qualities originating in his childhood days on his father's farm. Willie's powerful ambition and passion for risk taking, though, are his alone—as the reader will eventually discover.

After the awkwardly posed photographs of Willie have been taken, Willie's personal secretary, Sadie Burke, who had been traveling in the reporters' car, informs Willie that a political storm is brewing. Judge Irwin has just announced in the evening paper his support for one of Willie's political opponents. Energized by the news, Willie swings into action. He clears out the reporters and tells Jack to accompany him to pay a late night visit to Judge Irwin. Soon Jack is once more sitting in a speeding car, this time as it tears through the night to Burden's Landing, a small, well-to-do town 130 miles away on the Gulf Coast.

JUDGE IRWIN'S HOME

The last section of chapter 1 is filled with potent images of the aristocratic Old South, a society based on the prime cultural imperative of a clearly defined class structure. Since a class forms a hierarchy with the aristocrats at the top, the merchants and professionals in the middle, and the plain folk on the bottom, it suggests an ideal of perfectibility; that is, the higher up the scale, the more noble the person— or at least that is what the cultural myth proclaimed.

Judge Irwin, a southern gentleman from the old school, lives in Jack's hometown, Burden's Landing, a settlement named after Jack's ancestors. As the black limousine moves swiftly past the stately row houses Jack knows so well, memories of his past stir within him. In one house his mother, an aging southern belle, now lives with her latest husband. A little farther on is the Stanton house, where Adam and Anne, his childhood friends, lived. As they approach Irwin's white house, a brief memory rushes through Jack's mind of the judge as a proud figure on horseback; this memory is then followed by a flood of reminiscences about Jack's early friendship with Anne and Adam, his falling in love with Anne (his perfect southern belle), his hunting with the judge, and his putative father's deserting the family, which left the judge to become like a father to Jack.

Willie uses Jack to force an introduction with Judge Irwin, who remains disdainful of both of his visitors throughout the meeting as they argue about the upcoming senatorial campaign. Willie supports Masters, and Irwin has come out for Callahan. Sparks fly between the representative of the New South and his counterpart in the Old. Judge Irwin refuses to support Masters, because he has learned that the state senator has not been "responsible." Willie counters with the argument that all people are tainted with some foulness and all Willie can do is use the dirt to try to make a diamond. The judge, repelled by Willie's moral tone, maintains a stoic dignity in the face of the Boss's assault. In this combat of wills between the Old and the New South the reader witnesses a traditional moralist stand his ground against a modern relativist. The brief encounter results in a draw, with neither side vanquishing the other.

When the talk about the ethics of political endorsements becomes heated, the judge insists that Willie and Jack leave his home. Back in the car, rushing powerfully through the night, the Boss orders Jack to dig up some dirt on Judge Irwin. When Jack tries to tell Willie that the search will be a fool's errand, Willie orders him to look anyway, because everyone is corrupt and "There is always something" (49).

Jack tells the reader in the chapter's last paragraph that the events of the night he has just recounted happened "a good while ago" (49). In a stunning conclusion to this narrative sequence he then calls the roll, from the perspective of 1939, of the people who were alive three years earlier in 1936 but are now dead: Masters, Judge Irwin, Adam Stanton, and Willie Stark. Jack implies that the coming tragedy was the result of the "something" he found out about the judge. Thus, the first chapter ends with a skillfully crafted series of events and memories spaced out along a southern governor's hectic road trip through the kingdom he controls. Along the way the reader has met the main players, learned the major conflict, and discovered the author's narrative techniques.

6

The Early Campaigns and the Great Sleep

In chapter 2 Jack continues to use flashbacks and reminiscences to tell the reader about Willie's early career and eventual rise to the governorship of the state. Throughout most of these sequences Jack appears primarily as an objective observer, but he begins to let the reader see his personality in more depth. Still told from the perspective of 1939, chapter 2 covers the years from 1922 to 1930. It is structured around two of Willie's campaigns and a period of Jack's unemployment. The first two segments flow together logically through a normal chronological connection, and the last one, while at first seemingly unrelated, falls into place with a cause-and-effect relationship.

THE CAMPAIGN FOR COUNTY TREASURER

Warren divides old-style southern politicians, traditionally known as the good old boys, into two groups. The differences between the two interconnected groups are a matter more of degree than of kind. The first group Willie confronts is the local, or county, crowd—plain people who have weaseled their way into the public trough.

These local politicians deal with small-time matters, such as the award-ing of contracts for the rare public building. Since membership to county politics is based mainly on kinship, this group exists as a small, tightly controlled entity, characterized by narrow self-interest. The sec-ond layer of the good old boys is the state-level politicians, who are more experienced, more sophisticated, and more duplicitous than their country cousins. Since power in this group depends on the craftiness of the backroom politician to negotiate bribes and kickbacks, member-ship in this circle of self-serving pragmatists is more restrictive and dangerous than it is at the county level. Ultimately, though, both groups serve the same masters—the Old South aristocrats, from whose ranks come all the top leaders at the state level: the governors, sena-tors, and attorneys general. All in all, the political system is a well-oiled machine devoted to protecting the vested interests of those who adhere to the conservative standards of the Old South. There is no room in this scheme for anyone who would disrupt the status quo and attempt to initiate a new way of doing business in the state.

In chapter 2 the reader discovers how Willie overcomes the obstacles placed in his way by the good old boys and begins to under-stand the qualities in Willie's personality that allow him to move onto the political scene as something new under the state's sun. Like chap-ter 1, this chapter begins with an automobile trip to Mason City, but this time Jack travels alone in a Model-T Ford over a dirt road so rut-ted that it rattles his teeth. The year is 1922, and Jack has been sent to Mason City by the *Chronicle* to find out why Willie Stark, the county treasurer, has been making disturbing allegations about a school-bond issue. Once in Mason City Jack notices how slowly time passes in the town square. It is "the place where Time gets tangled in its own feet and lies down like an old hound and gives up the struggle" (52). It is an appropriate place for the plain folk to congregate. The languid pace of this gathering spot contrasts dramatically with the swiftly moving events after the son of the New South steps forward.

From the townspeople, Jack learns that Willie Stark has become a pariah because he has questioned a bid that was let by the county commissioners to build a new brick schoolhouse. From Willie, he dis-covers that the bid not only was the highest of those submitted but also was going to a construction firm that used an inferior grade of brick. In the ensuing conversation Jack and the reader come to understand a great deal about the mechanism of the good-old-boy system of politics in the county, in itself a microcosm of state politics. For one thing, Willie himself had been allowed to run for county treasurer only because he was a distant relative of the chairman of the Board of County Commissioners. In addition, Lucy has lost her job as a school-teacher because of Willie's opposition to the school contract. Along with the local sheriff, the chairman controls the whole county. Even in a dirt-poor, backwoods, unsophisticated place like Mason County the political structure is a cleverly managed oppressive machine run by only the few in power.

A new election is now coming up, and Willie is determined to run for reelection, even though he and Lucy know it is a hopeless cause. He enters the campaign but does so poorly that he almost becomes a comic figure. His chances are slim for two reasons. First, at this point in his career he is an ineffective public speaker, one who tries to explain rationally to his listeners just how crooked the school-house deal was and then bores them with facts and figures to support his arguments. Second, the county newspaper will neither cover his campaign nor print his handbills explaining his program. Nevertheless, Willie doggedly continues to campaign and make the rounds through-out his district until polling day, but to no avail.

After his inevitable defeat Willie returns to his father's farm and prepares for his next career move. During his failed campaign, though, he has learned how powerful a political machine can be, even in an insignificant place like Mason County. Without the support of the good old boys, he could not be elected to any post. The campaign does demonstrate, though, that Willie is no run-of-the-mill, backwoods politician. Something lies smoldering beneath the surface that has not yet been released. Whatever it is that makes Willie different has been hinted at in his stubborn determination to pursue a goal despite over-whelming odds.

While Willie earnestly believes he wants to be a leader of the people, he is personally insulted by the county politicians who dumped him. Lucy tells him, "Now, honey, you didn't want to be mixed up with them anyway. Not after you found out they were dishonest and crooked" (61). Willie replies sullenly, "They tried to run it over me. . . . Like I was dirt" (61). The part of Willie's personality that does not take bruises to his ego lightly will figure prominently in his future development.

THE CAMPAIGN FOR GOVERNOR

While working on his father's farm and selling Fix-It Household Kits door-to-door, Willie studies hard late at night to pass the state law board examination and eventually does pass it. Apparently headed for a mediocre career as a backcountry lawyer, Willie is suddenly thrust into the public limelight when, during a drill, the fire escape pulls loose from the schoolhouse that had been built with those "rotten" bricks Willie had warned the people about. Three children are killed; several more, seriously injured. Willie attends the triple funeral, where one of the bereaved fathers grabs his hand and shouts to the heavens, "Oh, God, I am punished for accepting iniquity and voting against an honest man!" (65). Willie's future in politics is now assured.

Willie's fame as a person concerned about the welfare of the common people spreads throughout the state, but for the moment he refuses to take advantage of it, preferring instead to bide his time. One day in 1926, though, he finds himself unexpectedly chosen by the Big Boys from the state capital to run for governor in the Democratic primary—the winner of which would almost automatically become governor, since at this time the South was virtually a one-party system. Suspicious at first but in the end too flattered to turn it down, Willie accepts the nomination and the limited support the party gives him and hits the campaign trail. Unfortunately for Willie, though, what he does not know is that one of the two factions in the party, the Harrison outfit, has decided to run Willie as a "dummy" to split the "hick" vote, thereby weakening support for the faction's opponents in the MacMurfee crowd. Later the party will regret ever coming up with such a scheme that tries to take advantage of a man like Willie Stark. Here again, as with the county machine, the reader sees just how manipulative a state political organization can be when it is controlled by a small, powerful group of insiders.

Initially Willie's second campaign is not much better than his first. While he does have a new suit and the halfhearted assistance of Tiny Duffy, one of Harrison's political hacks, as his campaign manager, Willie makes a sad spectacle touring the state in his secondhand car, giving the same dull speech over and over again, filled with tedious statistics and warmed-over platitudes derived from his reading the history of the lives of great people. Also—in what will prove to be a stroke of good luck—Sadie Burke, a bright woman knowledgeable about party politics, has been assigned to the Stark campaign by the party chiefs to handle his traveling and speaking arrangements. Jack, whose newspaper has sent him out to cover the campaign, finds the whole scene ludicrous. When he hears Willie practicing his speech at night in the hotel room next door, he has to stifle his laughter over the "poor half-witted bastard and his speech" (70). Nevertheless, both Jack and Sadie, who think of him as a "sap," also discern a hidden power in Willie that the puppetmasters in the capital cannot suspect— an abiding stubbornness and a relentless spirit that speak of some deep potential as yet unrealized.

Finally, in a hotel room in Upton on the night before the barbecue that will cap Willie's gubernatorial campaign, Sadie reveals to Willie how he has been used by the Harrison faction. When Jack confirms the frame, Willie is stunned. He takes a large drink of whiskey and proceeds to get drunk for the first time in his life. The next day a badly hungover Willie faces the crowd on the fairgrounds. He starts to deliver his stale speech when he suddenly stops, looks coldly determined, and erupts into a hellfire-and-brimstone harangue that stuns the crowd. He then resigns from the campaign and assigns his support to the opposition candidate, MacMurfee. Sadie, on the sidelines, has just decided that this "sap" is someone to take very seriously indeed.

Of all the characters in the novel, Sadie Burke is the one who speaks most frankly to the Boss. And of all the women, she is the one whose career most resembles that of Willie Stark. Growing up poor, her pasty white face pockmarked with scars from a childhood disease, Sadie learned quickly that the only way she would succeed was to assert herself aggressively in a man's world. She is the one who first notices Willie's special powers, and she has the savvy to link her career to his. Without Sadie's help in managing his career and without her political know-how, Willie would not have risen so rapidly and learned how to handle the affairs of state quite so well. To a large extent Sadie is responsible for the creation of the Boss, and he rewards her with the position of executive assistant when he becomes governor.

Sadie is, however, more than an opportunist taking advantage of a fortunate situation she happened to fall into. She is genuinely knowledgeable about the machinery of state politics, and beneath her tough, cynical exterior lies a woman capable of giving her heart to the man she loves. Later in the novel the reader learns that Sadie is a realist in affairs of the heart, forgiving Willie for his extramarital dalliances with showgirls and secretaries because she knows they offer no real threat to her status as Willie's lover. Her fatal mistake is in assuming that the Boss would not become serious about an aristocratic woman of the Old South like Anne Stanton or that he would not return to his estranged wife. Because she will not accept Willie's rejection, Sadie's rage leads her to destroy the man she loves, and for her jealousy and revenge she pays a heavy price in suffering and isolation. Like Annabelle Trice in the Cass Mastern story, Sadie Burke comes to grief because she dared to love a man in an adulterous love affair.

At Upton Willie undergoes a metamorphosis from Cousin Willie, the good old plodder with high hopes, into Willie the gritty realist. As much for revenge as for altruistic reasons, Willie is galvanized to defeat those who betrayed the public. He addresses the crowds as "Friends, red-necks, and fellow hicks" and inflames them with barnyard imagery: "Nail up anybody who stands in your way. You hand me the hammer and I'll do it with my own hand. Nail 'em up on the barn door! And don't fan away blue-bottles with any turkey wing!" (94, 96). Willie learns well the rhetoric that touches the heart of his listeners. Politicians with such ability can bypass facts and issues and sway crowds to their will—and with that support comes power that can make demagogues saviors of their people if they use it for the common good or dictators if they choose to serve their own needs.

Willie has found an effective political style but, more important-
ly, has discovered a link between himself and the plain people that will
eventually send him to the Governor's Mansion. The stage is finally set
now for Willie to overcome the masters of the old ways of doing business in state politics.

THE GREAT SLEEP

After the 1926 election Willie returns to Mason City to practice
law and there awaits the 1930 election, when he announces his candi-
dacy against the incumbent, MacMurfee. Jack describes this third
campaign as "hell among the yearlings and the Charge of the Light
Brigade and Saturday night in the back room of Casey's saloon rolled
into one" (97). At this point in the narrative Warren, through Jack,
could have given the reader a blow-by-blow account of this boisterous
campaign instead of a few brief remarks, but to have done so would
be repetitious, since the reader has already seen Willie at his rabble-
rousing best.

Instead, the narrative shifts away from Willie to Jack in this last
portion of the chapter and by doing so foreshadows what will eventually occur in the latter half of the novel, as Jack slowly moves to the
center of the reader's attention. In this last segment of chapter 2 Jack
explains that at times he withdraws from the world by wrapping himself up in a cocoon of inactivity. He calls it "The Great Sleep," and this
particular one has a direct connection with Willie's gubernatorial campaign. Still working for the *Chronicle* in 1930, Jack is warned by his
editor that unless he becomes more enthusiastic in his articles about
their man MacMurfee, he will be fired. Refusing to wait for the ax to
fall, Jack quits his job as reporter and stops doing much of anything
but eating and sleeping. This sequence recalls the first of the chapter,
when Jack sat frozen in time in the town square at Mason City.

During this retreat from the world Jack's mind wanders over the
past, and the reader discovers that Jack has walked out on the responsible life twice before—once while working on his Ph.D. dissertation

(the Cass Mastern papers) and again when he left his wife Lois. In subsequent chapters Jack will develop these two narrative strands at length. For the moment, though, Jack is content to drift along in a hazy, aimless mood in which nothing really matters to him except an occasional visit to his childhood friend Adam Stanton, now a famous surgeon, and a dinner date or two with Anne Stanton, the lost love of his life. Nothing really interests Jack until one day a telephone call from Sadie tells him that Willie, now the governor and the Boss, wants to see him immediately. When Jack shows up at the capitol, Willie offers him a job, and when Jack asks what he will do, Willie simply replies, "Something will turn up" (109). Jack concludes this chapter with the foreboding thought, "He was right about that" (109).

Chapter 2 shows the reader through the chronological ordering of two political campaigns how Willie Stark changed from a well-intentioned but hapless candidate into a fire-breathing orator able to scorch the souls of the plain folk. Just as significantly, the reader has been given a lesson in how Willie's forceful personality can capture the loyalty of an astute campaign worker like Sadie and galvanize an intelligent person like Jack to arise from his depressive stupor. Jack began his Great Sleep when, by refusing to glamorize Willie Stark's opponent, he became unemployed, and he ceased his aimless drifting when he answered the call of the Boss. Now that he has become one of the king's men, his life will have purpose and direction, qualities it has not had for a long time.

At this point in the narrative the reader may be puzzled by two of the plot developments. For one, what is wrong with this bright person that would lead him to cut himself off from his past and lapse into a state of emotional catatonia? And for another, why has Jack Burden betrayed his family and friends by joining forces with the Boss? Jack is a scion of the Old South, but he has given his allegiance to a man bent on destroying the old order. Jack's character becomes even more of a riddle when it is made clear that he does not care about the Boss's political program—it is the Boss by his force of will who has saved Jack from himself, and it is he alone who fills Jack with a sense of responsibility.

Content to separate himself from his Old South heritage and committed to nothing in the New except the Boss, Jack thinks he is a free man when in fact he is a troubled person with only a marginal sense of purpose. If he really is so independent and self-reliant, why does he lapse into periodic slumbers with their complete abnegation of responsibility? Without Willie, Jack would be a hollow man.

From this point on, the reader will hear several different voices from Jack the narrator. At times the voice will be cynical, indifferent, spiteful, and pained, but the voice that speaks to the reader from the perspective of 1939 will be mature, compassionate, and self-assured. Thus, from early in the novel the reader knows that Jack has endured the forthcoming calamities and has learned to live at peace with himself.

7

Little Jackie and the Two Impeachment Efforts

Like chapter 2, chapter 3 of *All the King's Men* is ordered around three units of narration. In a reversal of chapter 2's pattern, however, the first part of this chapter focuses on Jack, while the next two center on Willie. As in earlier chapters, the separate units will prove to be as intimately connected as the lives of Jack and Willie are. Here the reader begins to see a pattern emerging: As the narrative weaves a web of connected strands, the lives of the players in the drama begin to interrelate in far-reaching and significant ways. No one in this novel stands apart, separate and alone; for every decision a single individual makes other people will pay the consequences eventually, often in pain and suffering not of their own making. Finally, then, the issue becomes one of responsibility: Will the person who caused the suffering accept his or her contribution to the tragedy?

JACK'S VISIT TO BURDEN'S LANDING

Except for the trauma of his father's departure, Jack has led a nearly idyllic childhood, nurtured by the Old South culture in

Burden's Landing. The large house in which his mother now lives is an elegant southern mansion filled with art objects and attractive furniture. In appearance his mother was and remains a stunning example of the beautiful southern lady of the manor house. After Mr. Burden left, Jack was surrounded by a number of elegant southern gentlemen— including Judge Irwin—who became his substitute fathers. Jack's aristocratic friends and neighbors formed a caring community of like-minded believers, and at an early age he fell in love with a beautiful southern belle from one of the noblest of the state's families. Yet not all was well in this southern version of the Garden of Eden. The reader already knows that Jack is emotionally crippled, that he has removed himself from his aristocratic class, and that he has lost a father and the only woman he has ever loved. As an adult working for the Boss of a New South, he thinks he has freed himself from the pain of past suffering and from the narrow, conservative community of Burden's Landing. But as the reader will soon discover, Jack's problems—and growth—are just beginning.

In the last part of chapter 2 the reader saw that Jack suffers from some deep psychological flaw that periodically sends him into a Great Sleep. He did not spring full-blown into adulthood with his smart-aleck attitude and general indifference about life; he is an intelligent person whose emotional life was somehow stifled when he was a child, fragile and vulnerable. By continuing to focus on Jack while his memories roam over his home this chapter provides important clues about the origins of his cynicism and occasional torpor.

Jack returns to Burden's Landing in 1933 to spend some time with his mother, whom he has not seen in several months. Over the years Jack fought with his mother and purposefully removed himself from her world. He returns home occasionally under an armed truce that always breaks out into open warfare, signaling an end to each of his visits. These arguments distress Jack as much as they do his mother, and recently Jack has come to sense that they are the result of an unknown issue they have never discussed. About their most recent quarrel, one over Jack's working for a man who represents a threat to his mother's way of life, Jack thinks, "There was a shadow taller and darker than the shadow of Willie standing behind us" (111). Thus, despite the bitter arguments blighting their relationship, Jack feels compelled to continue returning to his mother's home to complete some unresolved business or to understand some part of his life that does not make sense to him. While sitting in the living room of the elegantly furnished house with his mother and her present husband, whom Jack refers to disdainfully as "the Young Executive," he reviews in his memory his mother's series of husbands, and he notices how the furniture and the husbands keep changing, while his mother remains the same, aging slowly and flawlessly. Unlike Mr. Burden and the parade of stepfathers, Jack notes sadly, "I was the thing that always came back" (115). That his mother is a mystery to Jack is indicated in part by the fact that he never gives the reader her first name and only rarely mentions her husbands' last names. At this point the reader understands what Jack does not—that the absence of a real father has seriously affected his relationship with his mother and that somehow the emptiness in his life and his callousness about his stepfathers are matters he is going to have to come to terms with before he can become an emotionally whole, mature human being.

While walking on the beach one day, Jack thinks back to a picnic he went on there with Anne and Adam Stanton in the summer of 1915, when he was 17 and Anne was nearly 14. They had gone for a swim, and Jack noticed for the first time that he was attracted to Anne. The image of Anne floating on her back in the Gulf waters, her face turned to the sky, becomes an indelible memory that only glows brighter in his mind's eye as the years pass. Jack marks this "picnic I never forgot" as a turning point in his life (118). It is also the point at which Jack begins to elevate Anne onto the pedestal reserved for the fairest and purest of southern womanhood—the southern belle. To Jack Anne will become an object of adoration like that of the woman in Edgar Allan Poe's "To Helen"—and she will exemplify more than perfect beauty; she will symbolize the highest aspiration of southern *man*hood. In this Old South tradition woman becomes an abstraction that represents a pure spot of holy innocence in an otherwise broken and corrupt world. Just as it is with Poe's narrator who exclaims, "Ah, Psyche, from the regions which / Are Holy-Land," this moment is sacred to Jack because it marks the starting point of the happiest period in his life, and it signals the beginning of his own sense of identity as a unique human being—another important component he needs before he can grow up.

Jack remains with his mother for a few days until an argument over his behavior at a dinner party given by Judge Irwin sends him running back to the capital. On the new concrete highway, driving an automobile at night in the rain, he relaxes for the first time in days and re-creates a vision of his mother and father's first meeting. Ellis Burden, an aristocratic southern lawyer, had gone to a small lumber town in Arkansas to settle a lawsuit and, while there, fell in love with the beautiful blue-eyed daughter of a local store clerk. When he left on the train, she was in the seat next to him, holding his hand. Jack's mother, then, is a child of the plain folk. Her natural beauty had been her passport out of her rural community and into Burden's Landing. And like the heroine in the best traditions of the classical English novel, such as Charlotte Brontë's *Jane Eyre*, she has made this escape through marriage—the one permissible way for a woman to move up the rungs of the social ladder in a class society. Unlike Jane Eyre, though, this beautiful southern woman never loved her Mr. Rochester. Once more, as in the reconstruction of the earlier scenes about Willie and Lucy, Jack has invented an emotion-filled episode, but in the lives of other people. His own emotional life, though, remains a void.

The Attempt to Impeach Byram White

After Jack reaches the capital the reader witnesses several more scenes of the New South politician in action. Sadie informs Jack that "Hell has popped" and tells him to come to the Boss's hotel suite at once (130). There he discovers Byram White, the state auditor, cowering under a merciless diatribe from Willie Stark. That White has been caught taking bribes does not bother Willie so much as that he did so without Willie's knowledge and was stupid enough to get caught, thus inviting impeachment proceedings from the MacMurfee outfit in the legislature. Willie makes White grovel and write an undated resignation letter. After White slinks out of the room Willie tells Jack he is disappointed in White for showing no backbone while being humiliated. Willie's political acumen has now grown to an understanding of the motivations of his henchmen. As long as they are afraid, they can be controlled, but if they are cowed they can never be trusted. Jack watches the whole episode without the slightest sympathy for White and without blinking an eye at the Boss's cruelty.

Willie intends to stop the impeachment proceedings against White through blackmail, threats, and bribes—anything it takes to accomplish the task at hand. The ends justify the means. When Hugh Miller, his ethical attorney general and a member in good standing with the Old South rulers, threatens to resign over the way Willie is handling the Byram White affair, Willie maintains that he must protect White or the MacMurfee people will regain their power and the state will be worse off than it was before. A person of honor like Judge Irwin, Miller does not accept Willie's rationalization and resigns. When he walks out, Willie tells Jack that his wife, Lucy, is planning to do the same because she too cannot condone protecting a thief. Deeply bothered by this twin assault on his integrity from two different sides of the Old South culture, Willie resolves then and there to "build me the God-damnedest, biggest, chromium-platedest, formaldehyde-stinkingest free hospital and health center the All-Father ever let live" (139). Now that Miller and Lucy, the ones who represented honest government and family fidelity in his life, have departed, Willie attempts to compensate for their loss by creating a center devoted to healing humankind. As the reader will see later, even a modern facility like this will not be able to save Willie's life or his soul.

THE ATTEMPT TO IMPEACH WILLIE STARK

Once the MacMurfee people get wind of Willie's methods of halting the move to impeach White they turn on him for "attempting to corrupt, coerce, and blackmail the Legislature" (145). The Boss becomes energized, and with Sugar-Boy at the wheel, the reader goes on another wild and manicky automobile ride as Willie takes his case to the people: "He roared across the state at eighty miles an hour, the horn screaming, from town to town, crossroads to crossroads, five, six, or seven, or eight speakings a day" (145). Willie's routine is pure demagoguery now, as he incites the crowds to screaming responses and charges them to march on the capitol the day his impeachment vote will be taken. This accomplished orator now has the plain people just where he wants them, to serve as his tool to destroy the last remnants of the state's good old boys.

Behind the scenes Willie bribes and blackmails enough legislators to sign a document (a round-robin) stating they will not vote against him, and thus the outcome of the proceedings is a foregone conclusion. With a piece of paper, Willie wins the war before the battle is fought, and the good old boys with their aristocratic masters lose their monopoly on power. On the day of the vote the legislature is further intimidated by thousands of Willie's supporters who have gathered outside the capitol chanting, "Willie, Willie, Willie—We want Willie" (148). When a triumphant Willie addresses the crowd that night with the news that he will remain their governor, they believe they have made it all possible. Having vanquished the old-style politicians, Willie owes allegiance to no one. He stands alone with the "awful responsibility" of how to use the complete power that is now his.

The Boss is at the height of his political power. Since no one can touch him, his reelection to the governorship in 1934 is mentioned only in passing—"the Boss succeeded himself with a vengeance" (155). Yet not all is well in the Boss's domain. Along the way he has taken a series of mistresses, Sadie being one of them, and Lucy no longer lives with him. A plain country woman, Lucy deals with the corruption in the capital the only way she can, by retreating to her sister's poultry farm and holding steady in her faith in God and her love for an adulterous husband and her spoiled, undisciplined son, even though she does occasionally support Willie by turning up for publicity photographs, as she had done in the sequence in chapter 1 at Old Man Stark's farm.

Chapter 3 adds to the reader's understanding of the developing narration in two ways. First, Jack becomes more interesting as he tells about his past and indicates the origins of his present contempt for the world around him. Through his review of memories that will not go away, he is coming alive for the reader in a way he could never do were he to remain a bystander who just happened to be in the right place at the right time to record the actions of a powerful leader. He still has a long way to go to win the reader's sympathy, but at least he has made a start. Second, the reader sees Willie in a series of maneuvers that are exciting in their daring and audacity but also troubling in their disregard for decency and fair play. At the same time the reader's admiration for Willie is becoming ambivalent as he develops into a skillful manipulator, bending people to his will in both private and public confrontations. He has become a paradox; the more tightly he weaves his control over state politics, the more his family life unravels and the more his ethics become tattered.

8

Jack the Graduate Student and the Cass Mastern Story

Chapter 4 contains a structural development unusual in the modern novel—a framed story that appears to have no relevance to the main narrative. The chapter begins and ends with Jack as a graduate student working on his Ph.D. in 1920 and 1921. These two parts "frame" the larger, central project Jack is researching for his dissertation—the journals and letters of Cass Mastern, written 60 years earlier, during the Civil War period. At this point in the narrative Jack's graduate school days and especially the Cass Mastern episode have little bearing on the Willie Stark matter that so far has monopolized the reader's interest. It is worth noting, however, that two earlier parts of the novel—the Great Sleep and Jack's visit to Burden's Landing—shifted the reader's attention to the person who is telling the entire story. The movement away from Willie and toward Jack continues here, in this case with a complete chapter, not just a fragment of one. Later these narrative units will serve as valuable aids in Jack's developing understanding of the impact of the life of Willie Stark on "all the king's men and women."

One of the major points of the Mastern story is that the past actions in a person's life have a direct bearing on present and future events. And so it will be in the overall narrative. Whatever now puzzles the reader about this segment's relevancy will eventually be made clear, once Jack develops the prerequisite emotional insights to make the connections between his own past and present and between himself and Willie. Jack's inability to understand the Mastern story and his distancing of himself from the morality of his research for the Boss are both symptoms of an emptiness at the core of his being.

Jack in Graduate School

Jack notes that the Boss's request that he dig into Judge Irwin's past for information to use against him was a "proper assignment" for him, since he had once been a history student (157). He states, "It was to be my second excursion into the past, more interesting and sensational than the first, and much more successful" (157). His comment about how "successful" the second is will prove to be tragically ironic. The ultimate irony, of course, lies in the contradiction of Jack's being a historian who cares nothing about his own past.

Jack then begins to tell about his first excursion into the past, a journey that had been unsuccessful because, as he now knows, he had tried "to discover the truth and not the facts" (157). Since he could not or chose not to understand the results of his research, he walked away from it; only now, from the perspective of 1939, does he decide to reopen the old box of note cards and dust off the manuscript from graduate school for a new attempt at comprehension. The old story may appear to have little to do with Willie directly, but as Jack has come to believe, "it has a great deal to do with the story of Jack Burden, and the story of Willie Stark and the story of Jack Burden are, in one sense, one story" (157). Now Jack's involvement with Willie is beginning to appear more complex than it has so far. Perhaps his fascination with Willie goes beyond that of a loyal follower absorbed in the charismatic leader. In this chapter the narrator hints that in some other important way he and Willie are very similar, despite the differences in their family backgrounds, education, and class origins.

As Jack begins the recitation of his graduate school days, he changes the literary point of view from first to third person as a way of emphasizing how different he is now from the way he was then. By calling himself "Jack Burden" instead of "I" he lets the reader know that he now considers his curious behavior as a graduate student to be something remote and detached from his real self. Jack the graduate student was playing a role in a perverse drama he had scripted without understanding why, except perhaps to punish himself, his mother, and his wife for reasons he did not then understand.

Jack used his college career to force the break between himself and his parents' generation that had nurtured him and to enter the modern, disconnected generation of the New South. Everything he did was designed to erase the memories of his origins by destroying his ties with his mother, his wife, and his few remaining friends from Burden's Landing. While working toward his Ph.D. in American history at the state university (presumably Louisiana State University), Jack lived like a bum in a run-down apartment with two other pathetic students who would be well on their way to becoming alcoholics had their stipends as graduate assistant teachers not been so meager. They are indifferent to their studies and have no interest in their future careers. Jack, though, relishes living in their cockroach-infested dump with his hopeless companions, especially when his mother visits and has to see him in such squalor. She had wanted to pay for his education in an Ivy League school, probably Princeton or Yale, where aristocratic southern men were sent, but Jack had rejected her offer and decided to work his way through the plain folks' school to spite her. He thought she just wanted to be able to brag to her upper-class friends about where her son was going to college.

Once Jack's mother sent him a check for $250 to buy some decent clothes but he "did not even buy a necktie" (159). Instead, he used it to finance a "blowout" for himself and his roommates. The result of their binge was that one of the roommates contracted a venereal disease, and the other subsequently lost his job and disappeared from campus. Jack, however, remained "invulnerable" to the whole episode; perhaps, he says, that was "the curse of Jack Burden," to remain untouched by surrounding events (159). Jack has certainly proved this to be the case in the way he treats his mother with disdain and his roommates with indifference. By consciously irritating his mother with his obnoxious behavior and by carelessly providing his roommates with the means for their destruction Jack is unknowingly training himself for the insensitivity that will serve him well when he follows the Boss's orders to uncover scandals in the lives of political opponents. By the time Jack gets to work on his good friend (and real father) Judge Irwin he will be eminently qualified for the task.

As a graduate student, Jack distanced himself from the concerns of the present by exploring the past, and that meant the letters and diaries of Cass Mastern, Ellis Burden's maternal uncle. At this point in his life Jack does not know that Judge Irwin is his real father and that he and Cass are therefore not blood kin. When he finally discovers this fact, though, it will not matter anyway, since his life and Cass Mastern's will have become closely entwined, even at a distance of more than 50 years. And before the novel is over the reader will be convinced that the stories of Cass Mastern, Willie Stark, and Jack Burden are indeed just one story.

THE CASS MASTERN STORY

The Cass Mastern story is set in the historical period in which the Old South reigned (1820–65). It was the time during which the South developed most of the cultural traits that would endure well into the twentieth century and deeply influence the lives of people like Jack Burden. The concepts of a landed gentry, the lord and lady of the manor house, the southern belle, honor, noblesse oblige, the plantation, and gracious living all became part of the southern dream of the good life during this time. In the events transpiring in this story the ideas of freedom and responsibility are explored in terms of a region's social standards, its unique experience with chattel slavery, and its defeat in a civil war. Nowhere else in the novel do the South's most important moral issues of slavery and racism play such significant roles. Thus, the narrative of Cass Mastern serves as a parable of the rise and fall of the historical Old South.

Cass Mastern, along with his brother Gilbert and his sister Lavinia, were plain people born into poverty in a log cabin in the red-clay hill country of northern Georgia. Gilbert ran away to Mississippi, where he worked his way up to the plantation aristocracy by 1850. After making his fortune he returned to Georgia, placed Lavinia in an Atlanta finishing school, and brought Cass to live with him at Valhalla, his plantation in Mississippi.

Cass entered Transylvania College in Lexington, Kentucky, and quickly learned the finer points of gambling, drinking, and whoring. He also became friends with Duncan Trice, a young, fun-loving banker who joined him in some of these pursuits—at least the drinking and gambling, for Duncan was faithful to his wife, whom he dearly loved. Duncan brought Cass home to meet his wife, Annabelle, and Cass became immediately infatuated with the woman, who thrilled him to the depths of his soul. When he looked into her eyes for the first time, he was nearly overwhelmed by the physical sensations that flooded his body. The culture of the Old South encouraged the loyalty and friendship between Cass and Duncan, and both men, according to their traditions, looked on the beautiful Annabelle as the most valuable portion of their lives. Trouble arose, however, when southern male friendship came into conflict with the southern belle.

Over the next year Cass visited the Trice mansion often, and eventually he and Annabelle began a passionate love affair, made even more exciting because it betrayed not only the marriage vows but also the cultural mores of friendship and hospitality. Cass was incredulous that he could embrace the wife of his "friend and benefactor" in the husband's own house (169). But the sexual attraction was impossible to resist. Later, after the affair had reached its tragic conclusion, Cass decided that a person cannot claim any virtue until that person has faced an overwhelming temptation—a point that will subsequently haunt Jack Burden in his love affair with Anne. And later in the novel these scenes of wild desire between Cass and Annabelle will stand in marked contrast to Jack and Anne's love relationship, with its missed chance at high passion.

Cass and Annabelle's affair raged for a year and a half; all the while Cass and Duncan hunted, gambled, and drank together as the best of friends. Then in March 1854 Duncan Trice was found dead in his library, with a bullet in his chest, ostensibly the victim of a gun-cleaning accident. Cass was one of the pallbearers. On the night of the funeral he met Annabelle in the summerhouse, where they kissed cold-ly, after which Annabelle placed Duncan's wedding ring on Cass's fin-ger. Phebe, a beautiful woman and Annabelle's personal slave, had found the ring on Annabelle's pillow and given it to her. Like many of the other slaves, Phebe had known about their affair, and she under-stood that Duncan had placed the ring on the pillow so that Annabelle would know he had committed suicide. Annabelle, horrified that Phebe knew the truth, sold her "down the river" for $1,300, which she gave to an old blind black man in a futile attempt to assuage her guilt (176).

Annabelle suffers remorse for her part in the death of her hus-band and the sorrowful fate of her servant, but she will not endure the constant reminder of that guilt, even if it means losing the man she loves. Ironically, both women, white mistress and black slave, have been drawn into misery by what other people read in their eyes. Through her aggressive sexuality and her awareness of guilt, Annabelle Trice becomes more than the stereotypical southern belle on which her portrait is based; she is a character who suffers the consequences of her flawed humanity.

Cass was overwhelmed by the horror of the chain of events that resulted from their affair—the betrayal of his friend, the suicide, the selling of Phebe, and now the end of his love for Annabelle. As the burden of his guilt grew, his world began to fall apart, and he conclud-ed that the entire calamity was the result of his "single act of sin and perfidy" (178). His action had set up a "vibration" in the "whole fab-ric of the world" and had "spread infinitely and with ever increasing power and no man could know the end" (178). By not acting respon-sibly he has managed to destroy his life and that of others around him.

In near despair over the fate of Phebe, Cass returned to Mississippi, ran his plantation, read his Bible, prayed for salvation, prospered, and freed his slaves. But his subsequent attempt to run the plantation with wage-earning free blacks failed, and he had to send them up North, where he knew they would not fare much better. Cass could not stand for them to look at him in their misery and remind him of Phebe. Although he no longer condoned slavery, his brother Gilbert did. Gilbert was a man who could "retain enough of innocence and strength" to do a "little justice in the terms of the great injustice," a description that could just as well apply at times to Willie Stark and Jack Burden (184). Unlike Cass and Jack, Gilbert and Willie accept the limitations of human nature and at least make an attempt to improve the human condition.

Cass joined the Confederate army when the Civil War began, though not as an officer as he could have done, given his education and status, but as a private. He was determined to march in the ranks, wearing his friend's wedding ring on a chain around his neck and carrying a musket he would never fire at an enemy. In his journal he recorded, "How can I who have taken the life of a friend, take the life of an enemy, for I have used up my right to blood" (186). Cass witnessed some of the worst battles of the war, waiting for a bullet to end his life, until finally in a battle near Atlanta he was wounded in the leg. He died a slow, agonizing death in a hospital in 1864, content that God had forgiven him. In the end Cass expiated his guilt over his irresponsible acts and died a free man, finally aware of his own inadequacies and accepting the flawed human condition. His story, from his birth in poverty through his ascendancy to wealth and graceful living to his death in warfare, has also been a fair approximation of the region's history from 1830 to 1865.

Jack's Departure from Graduate School

After Jack has given the reader the story of Cass Mastern, he returns to "Jack Burden" and his attempt to make sense of the papers in graduate school. He had studied the Mastern papers for a year and a half and finally come to realize that "he did not know Cass Mastern" (188). And even though he had completed enough work on the historical document to take his doctorate, he refused to write it all up, thereby illustrating once more his inability to act in a responsible manner. Instead, he stared at Cass's photograph by the hour and wrote not a word.

Jack then returns to the present of 1939 to explain why Jack the graduate student could not understand Cass Mastern. Cass had learned that "the world is all of one piece," like "an enormous spider web" (188). A touch in one part is felt throughout the web, and the spider, like God, may exact a heavy penalty. Cass's spiderweb image is an excellent metaphor for the complexity of human responsibility. As a 23-year-old graduate student, Jack could not understand Cass's story, for to do so would have meant admitting that his own life was deeply flawed, and this he was unwilling to do. To avoid the issue Jack entered one of his Great Sleeps, until one day he simply walked away from the "slatternly" apartment, leaving Cass's writings behind. His landlady gathered them up and shipped them to him, and for years he carried the yellowing parcel around unopened, through a succession of apartments, furnished rooms, and hotels. When he now comes back to the papers in 1939, he is prepared to interpret the "darkness and trouble" that had blighted the fated life of Cass Mastern (165). By now Jack has endured his own portion of darkness and trouble and come to much the same conclusions about human life as Cass had.

Chapter 4 prepares the reader for the novel's subsequent developments in two important ways. First, the reader sees Jack as a talented researcher more than capable of uncovering the hidden facts in a person's life. For example, Cass Mastern never mentioned Annabelle or Duncan Trice by name in his journals, but Jack, noticing the date of Duncan's death, tracked down a newspaper account that covered the fatal "accident" and came up with their names. Jack's skill as a researcher has already served the Boss well, but his gift will lead him to disaster when applied to his next project. One of the ironies in Jack's life is that he is a good investigator when it comes to other people's lives, but he cannot or will not make sense out of his own past. This factor will cease to be a problem when his next historical project, look-ing into Judge Irwin's past, actually becomes his own story.

Second, in the Cass Mastern journals the reader follows a version of one of the oldest stories in the literature of the Western world—the love triangle based on adultery. It was a classic when Lancelot and Guinevere betrayed King Arthur, and it is as contemporary as the lat-est television soap opera. During the nineteenth century variations on this story informed most of the popular fiction of the South in hun-dreds of plantation and sentimental romances. Although told and retold thousands of times, the adulterous love story shows no signs of losing its power to fascinate reading and viewing audiences. While the reader has already seen in chapter 3 that Willie has begun to take a series of lovers, Willie's love life has been developed only briefly, to illustrate how jealous his mistress Sadie can become when she learns about one of Willie's latest "tarts." In this chapter, however, the Cass-Annabelle- Duncan love triangle moves the reader to consider the trag-ic consequences of an adulterous love affair in terms of betrayal, misery, and death. The suffering caused by Cass and Annabelle's adul-tery serves as a template by which to measure three more love triangles that Jack will tell the reader about before he closes his story. And each one will illustrate the tragedy of irresponsible behavior in human rela-tions.

9

The Case of the Upright Judge

In chapter 5 the reader begins to discern a moral corruption behind the facade of propriety and manners in the contemporary traditions of the Old South. The twentieth-century inheritors of the Old South's values are men and women whose lives appear to be highly honorable and eminently just but in reality are something far different. Like Cass Mastern and Annabelle Trice, fashionable ladies and gentlemen, such as Mrs. Burden, Judge Irwin, and Governor Stanton, have also committed adultery and betrayed their fellow human beings. And like Cass, they too prove to be capable of heroic sacrifice to expiate the guilt of their sins. Warren insists that these people are not unfeeling hypocrites or evil characters; they are ordinary human beings who have made terrible mistakes and are eventually capable of accepting the consequences of their misdeeds. Nevertheless, the modern generation, Jack, Anne, and Adam—their sons and daughters—are devastated by the knowledge that their elders have not been the perfect ideals of southern man- and womanhood that they have always expected them to be. How success-ful the children are in dealing with the shocking truth about their par-ents will depend on their ability to free themselves from the past and their willingness to accept responsibility for their own lives.

Chapter 5 loops back to the end of chapter 1 to pick up the "present-time" narrative in 1936, after the late-night visit to Judge Irwin's, when the Boss told Jack to dig up some dirt on the judge. Between chapters 1 and 5 the reader has learned how events in the past have helped shape the personalities of Willie and Jack. As the reader returns to the main narrative, he or she goes armed with an understanding of Willie's idea about the derivation and use of power and of Jack's inability to accept responsibility. Jack's first research project left him unconcerned and unmoved; this time, however, when Jack carries out the governor's orders, he will alter his life and the lives of others drastically as he achieves "a sensational success" with his second lengthy historical project. Consequently, he will lose his moral indifference and emotional aloofness.

Telling his story in the first person again, Jack gives the reader five units of narration in this chapter. The longer ones—"The Scholarly Attorney," "The House of Governor Stanton," and "The Judge and the Power Company"—all merge together as an interconnected story that chronicles Jack's historical investigation he now calls the "Case of the Upright Judge." Interspersed among these are two shorter pieces—"Tom the Sophomore Thunderbolt" and "Tiny Duffy and the Hospital Contract"—in which Jack briefly views a couple of matters that will grow in importance as the narrative continues to unfold.

THE SCHOLARLY ATTORNEY

Jack insists that he will be unable to find out anything about Judge Irwin that the Boss can use to ensure the election of his senatorial candidate, but Willie understands Jack and human nature well enough to know that Jack will do a good job for him and that he will eventually unearth something. And the next day, mildly troubled by investigating a friend, but confident he will find nothing, Jack sets out "to dig up the dead cat" (192). Before telling the reader any more about the search, he states ominously, "I found it," thereby piquing the reader's interest and proving the Boss's severe judgment about human nature was right all along (192).

Jack now takes the reader on a complex journey to locate the truth that has long been "buried under the sad detritus of time" (193). Always logical, Jack deduces that if there has been any wrongdoing in the judge's past, it must involve money, and the plausible starting point is to question the judge's onetime best friend, Jack's own father, Ellis Burden, or the "Scholarly Attorney," as he mockingly calls him. The irony of Jack's reasoning is that he has dismissed the notion that the judge could have had a problem with a woman. This logical flaw will be made dramatically clear to Jack later.

Although Jack detests the way his father left his mother and even more the way he has chosen to conduct his life, he has kept up with the man over the years, visiting him occasionally and arguing with him about religion. Jack knows that the Scholarly Attorney lives over a Mexican restaurant in the poor section of the city, where he preaches his fundamentalist religion and administers to the needs of the "unfortunate" (196). As Jack waits in the restaurant for his father's return from his street ministry, he learns that the Mexican owners of the establishment consider Mr. Burden a saint, but Jack thinks the man is "loco" (195). Once in the Scholarly Attorney's apartment Jack watches as his father takes care of his latest "unfortunate," an ex-aerialist from the circus who lost his mind when his wife, costumed as an angel, fell to her death during one of their performances. An odd story, the aerialist's experience will reverberate in the lives of Jack Burden and Adam Stanton when their "angel" Anne "falls" and the two men lose their minds.

While observing Mr. Burden carefully feeding the pitiful human being, who is so afraid of heights that he will not even stand up on the floor, Jack has a flashback to a time in his childhood when his father fed him by hand in much the same way. A surge of emotion wells up in Jack and forces him to whisper the word "Father" (200). The old man does not hear him distinctly, and the moment passes. But even if Jack does quickly dismiss the feeling, the incident does not go unnoticed by the reader, who sees for the first time that underneath his shell of cynicism Jack is capable of genuine and tender emotions. Jack's personality may not be so indifferent and irresponsible after all.

Jack questions the Scholarly Attorney about his "old bosom pal" Judge Irwin, but the old man refuses to give Jack a straight answer about the judge and does not care to discuss anything from what he calls his "sinful" past, filled, as he says, with "vanity and corruption" (201). To Jack all of this talk about sin and damnation is just more evidence that his father is crazy, but the reader should note that much of what Mr. Burden says echoes several passages in the Cass Mastern story. It is beginning to appear that Cass and Mr. Burden share a similar experience, especially the part after Cass's breakup with Annabelle.

Growing increasingly irritated as he hammers away at his father, Jack finally gets the Scholarly Attorney to exclaim that he will not talk about Irwin and "the world of foulness again" (202). Jack begins to suspect that the old man's words are not just jargon from a street preacher but a coverup for some damaging evidence in the past. Jack is correct and not only in the way he suspects. Disgusted with the old man, Jack leaves, convinced that something is wrong in the judge's past and that "Sooner or later" he will find it out (203).

Jack's relationship with his father is disturbing for several reasons. Not only does it show a son being disrespectful to his father, but also it shows that Jack's disdain for his father is so deep-seated that he can mock his father's ministry to the poor people in the city. By cynically dismissing the old man as a fool, Jack does not have to try to understand what brought his father to lead such a self-sacrificing existence. Were he not so indifferent to his father, perhaps he would notice that both the son and the father are alike in their rejection of their Old South heritage. And had he read the Cass Mastern story with more understanding, he might now begin to see the parallel between the lives of Cass and Mr. Burden.

TOM THE SOPHOMORE THUNDERBOLT

In this interlude Jack introduces the reader to Tom Stark, Willie's son and now a star quarterback for the state university football team. Willie is extravagantly proud of the handsome young athlete and screams enthusiastically when his "All American" leads his team to victory. If Willie is to be a prime mover of the New South, his son will be one of its finest representatives. Referring to Tom's athletic prowess, Willie shouts during one game, "he's a fast son-of-a-bitch!" but the comment leads Jack to declare forebodingly, "He was fast and he was a son-of-a-bitch," in regard to Tom's off-the-field behavior (204). Willie and the public are spoiling the Sophomore Thunderbolt with their adulation, and Tom's extracurricular activities with "bottle and bed" threaten to weaken his athletic performance. Willie loves his son dearly and wants him to have everything he was denied as a young man—fast cars, stylish clothing, women, and high times at roadhouses. Tom has already become an arrogant lout, but his father dotes on him and refuses to see what is happening to the boy—that he is becoming a self-centered brat with no ties to any cultural tradition and consequently with no strength of character at all. Given too much freedom, Tom has failed to develop any sense of responsibility. Lucy understands what is happening; however, her pleas to Willie to discipline their son only widen the rift that has developed between them. Before long Willie's plans for his son lead to serious trouble.

THE HOUSE OF GOVERNOR STANTON

A major characteristic of the culture of the Old South was a deep faith in the strong and honorable family. Normally patriarchal, the southern family was traditionally an institution an individual could depend on in good times and bad. The enduring family became a special mark of pride in the South during the difficult years following the Civil War. If the region could not yet compete nationally in politics or in the marketplace, perhaps it could develop certain spiritual areas of life—such as devotion to family—to compensate for its lack of material wealth. In some cases the idealization of the southern family gave way to ancestor worship, a practice that placed enormous pressures on its adherents.

Anne and Adam Stanton are two such true believers in the religion of family worship. Their god is their deceased father, Governor Stanton, whose spiritual presence has motivated them to become near-saints in the service of their fellow human beings. But what happens, Warren asks, to ancestor worshipers when they discover their god is merely another flawed human being? Jack will provide the means for the answer to this question and will eventually discover that his own emotional sickness also has something to do with the truth about his real father.

Back on the trail to find "the dead kitty in the ash heap," Jack agrees to spend a weekend with Anne and Adam Stanton at their old home in Burden's Landing, where they have gone together for a rare moment of relaxation. In the living room Jack watches Anne, in a ritual akin to an act of worship, kneel to light the wood in the fireplace, above which hangs a portrait of the formidable Governor Stanton. Anne and Adam loved and admired their father deeply, and all of their adult lives they have been trying to live up to the high standards they think he set for them. Adam drives himself mercilessly at his medical practice, taking care of the poor without pay and denying himself any meaningful private life. Anne does charity work throughout the city but still feels that she is not doing enough. In a sense her life is as empty as Jack's, a situation made worse by the fact that she is a woman living in a culture that does not expect her to fulfill herself in a role outside the home.

As Anne lights the fire, she laughs in a "sudden throaty, tingling way," so delighting Jack that the reader thinks he is in love with her (206). This suspicion is verified later, as Jack becomes upset when Anne tells him she had lunch with Governor Stark the previous week. Further, when she claims she has never done anything worthwhile, Jack says, "You could have married me," indicating that their relationship had at one time been more than a simple friendship (210). Jack appears to be disturbed that the pure and sweet southern belle of his youth and the daughter of one of the fine old aristocratic governors of the state would actually allow herself to be seen in the company of the tough, realistic new governor, a man who is not afraid to get his hands muddy when he makes political bricks. Jack's attitude is either overly protective or hypocritical, or perhaps both. He fears that the New South might contaminate the last remaining portion of innocence from his Old South past, and he resents it.

Just as he had done with the Scholarly Attorney, Jack begins to probe other people he has loved for information about Judge Irwin's past financial affairs. Anne dismisses the inquiries as a nuisance, but Adam in complete innocence reveals that the judge was indeed once broke. He had heard his father and the judge discussing a problem with money sometime around 1913 or 1914. The issue is dropped, and the old friends have a wonderful time in one another's company for the remainder of the evening. But Jack knows now that he has a solid piece of information about the judge that he can pursue with confidence. His questioning of his father and two childhood friends about another close friend, with only an occasional twinge of conscience, illustrates once more just how bankrupt Jack is morally and emotionally. That he takes a perverse delight in the task shows once more how bitter he is about the old order. And that it would please him to discover criminality among the elite proves how desperate he is to justify his own defection from their ranks.

TINY DUFFY AND THE HOSPITAL CONTRACT

Like Cass Mastern's spiderweb theory of human relationships, the seemingly unimportant action in this small scene will have far-reaching consequences in later events in the narrative. Through a few short paragraphs, Jack sketches a conversation he heard between Tiny Duffy and Sadie Burke about the $6 million contract to be let to build the new free state hospital and medical center. Tiny dreams of the possibilities of using the contract for political gain by throwing the contract to Gummy Larson as a way of undermining MacMurfee's support in the legislature. Sadie warns Tiny to stay away from the deal, and the matter is left hanging. By now, though, the reader should know that Jack is not going to introduce a portion of dialogue like this and let it casually fade from the narrative. For one thing, the reader has already followed the consequences of an earlier bid for a building contract that eventually catapulted Willie into the forefront of state politics. Gummy Larson, like Tom Stark, will return in later episodes to play his part in the tragedy of Willie Stark.

THE JUDGE AND THE POWER COMPANY

"'Smarty,' she said, 'smarty, you thought you were smart!'"
Thus, Anne informs Jack what she thinks of him when she calls to let
him know that Judge Irwin had solved his financial problem in the past
by marrying a wealthy woman. She hangs up the phone happy to have
put an end to Jack's investigation, and for a moment Jack too is
relieved to learn that the judge is clean—but only for a moment. As
Jack has told the reader, he is very good at his job, and his tenacity as a
researcher will not permit him to drop the matter so easily satisfied to
let the judge off the hook. He now plunges into the most complicated
bit of sleuthing in his career. Energized by the challenge, he has cleverly rationalized the intellectual pursuit of truth as a defense to carry out
the will of the Boss, such work giving him his only purposeful direction in life. If he cannot measure up to the ideals of his heroes, he is
determined to bring them down to his level. What Willie has done to
the Old South by rendering it politically impotent Jack will do to it
spiritually and morally.

From county courthouse records, he learns that the judge paid off
a substantial mortgage on his plantation in March 1914; from an old
newspaper, that the judge had married Mabel Carruthers in January
1914; and from a judgment docket book, that Mabel was in debt when
she married the judge, a fact confirmed by an ancient, wheelchair-
bound banker who had made loans to Mabel. Mabel therefore was pen-
niless when she married, and Jack again suspects that something is
"very, very hollow" in the judge's past (219). Jack recalls that the judge
had been the state attorney general under Governor Stanton but had
resigned in 1915 to take a job as vice-president with the American
Electric Power Company at an unusually high salary. But since the
mortgage had been paid in 1914, where had the money come from? In
an attempt to pursue this angle Jack purchases one share of stock in the
American Electric Power Company so that he can be admitted to exam-
ine the company's records as a concerned shareholder.

Searching through the company records, Jack discovers that the
judge had owned and sold a large chunk of the power company stock
in 1914. But how had the judge acquired the stock to begin with?

Through further digging in state records, Jack finds out that the judge, when he was the attorney general, had settled out of court a lawsuit over the use of public coal lands in favor of a private firm, the Southern Belle Fuel Company—a business connected to the American Electric Power Company through a parent corporation in New York City. Now Jack can make a shrewd guess about how the judge came into possession of the stock and received the fancy job, but he has no way of proving it—no way, that is, until it dawns on him to follow up regarding a thin lead on the death of Mr. Mortimer L. Littlepaugh, onetime counsel for the power company. A newspaper account of Littlepaugh's death in a fall from a fifth-story hotel balcony is filled with ambiguities, and so Jack tracks down the dead man's sister, Miss Lily Mae Littlepaugh.

After abusing her verbally Jack softens up Miss Littlepaugh and succeeds in bribing her to tell the truth about her brother's death. She then explains that Mortimer Littlepaugh was forced out of the company so that his position could go to Irwin. Mortimer took his case to Governor Stanton, who refused to act on the charges that his attorney general had been bribed by the power company. In despair Mortimer Littlepaugh committed suicide. With a photographic copy of the suicide note, Jack now has all the dirt he needs to bury the judge—and even more, he has also learned of the noble Governor Stanton's complicity in the sordid affair. At this point a more responsible and compassionate person might have dropped the whole matter, especially since the crimes indict people who love him. But Jack is too much the Boss's man to act on his own, and in a perverse way, by serving the Boss's needs he serves his own as well.

The main thrust of chapter 5 is to show Jack as the clever historical researcher in the process of finding out something disreputable in Judge Irwin's past. While Jack's service for the Boss advances the plot dramatically, several other issues have been introduced that will grow as the story progresses—among them Jack's relationship with his father, Anne's contact with Governor Stark, Adam's role as a medical specialist, and Tiny's involvement with Gummy Larson. At the same time Willie has been absent from the plot, but his presence always lurks in the background. And finally, throughout the research on the judge's past Jack has been excited by the challenge of his quest, and he takes a momentary delight in discovering that two of his heroes, Irwin and Stanton, have feet of clay—a realization that morbidly appeases his own low self-esteem. Now the reader understands an important reason for Jack's and Willie's being so much alike and for Jack's having given his allegiance to the Boss. Both men are set on destroying the old regime—but for very different reasons, one for revenge and the other for power—and both need the other to achieve this goal. Jack needs Willie's strength, and Willie needs Jack's intelligence.

10

Dr. Stanton and the Willie Stark Hospital

The events in chapter 6 are for the most part concurrent with Jack's search for a scandal in Judge Irwin's life, and the central purpose of the chapter is to show how the energetic New South can appropriate the Old through the Boss's appointment of Adam Stanton as the director of the soon-to-be-built Willie Stark Hospital. As in the preceding chapters, several smaller vignettes expand on earlier episodes, but one of them proves so devastating to Jack's psyche that it leaves him numb for days and rearranges the way he looks at the world.

TOM'S CAR CRASH

The chapter that is going to be about finding a director for a hospital begins appropriately with a short sequence that takes place primarily in a hospital. Tom Stark is recovering from a concussion he received when he smashed up his expensive yellow roadster while driving drunk. No charges are filed against the governor's son, of course, and Tom soon recovers from his injury, which turns out to have been relatively minor. The same, though, cannot be said for his companion, a pretty young blonde named Caress Jones, who will never be pretty again. Her father, the owner of a trucking business, threatens to expose the whole affair as a scandal, but a warning from Willie's associates about state contracts for his trucking firm shuts him up. Through the Boss's power, Tom has been protected from prosecution and a potential threat to Willie's popular image has been averted.

While Tom lies unconscious in the hospital emergency room, Willie and Lucy argue bitterly about Tom's future. Lucy pleads with Willie to put an end to their son's escapades, but Willie insists that to do so would make him a "sissy" and he wants Tom to have the "fun" he himself never had while growing up (230). The reader has already seen a similar confrontation between Willie and Lucy, but as the rift between them continues to grow, the trouble Tom gets into becomes more serious. The mother is powerless to stop the father, who will have his way no matter what. Willie arrogantly believes that he and his son are invincible and that all threats to their preeminence can be dealt with through bodily stamina and strength of will.

The Offer

Again the reader sees what Willie is capable of doing when he sets his mind to it. Having told his constituents he was going to build them a wonderful new hospital, Willie sets out to do just that, equipped with a single-minded determination that becomes an obsession. By traveling all over the country and studying the best hospitals he soon becomes an expert in what it takes to build a top-notch medical facility. He is at his organizational best with a project like this, and with his energy, devotion to detail, and zeal he reveals a positive side of his nature that the reader has not seen in some time. In reporting the Boss's devotion to the new project Jack too notices Willie's unusual determination to make the hospital perfect in every way. Not only must the hospital be large and modern, but Willie adamantly insists that the construction contracts and the hospital administration be completely free from the politics he knows would corrupt the pure and noble concept of the "Willie Stark Hospital."

While part of Willie wants the hospital as a monument to his memory, deep in Willie the admirable yearning to improve the lot of the plain people still burns.

In one scene Jack walks in on the Boss excoriating Tiny Duffy, who has again tried to get the governor to throw the main building contract to Gummy Larson in return for political favors. Willie will not stand for any deal making in the construction of his hospital, and he does not want Tiny or Gummy to lay a finger on the project, despite Larson's being an excellent contractor. Willie's harsh verbal attack leaves Tiny sweating and frightened. After Willie commands Tiny to leave he tells Jack that in order to make his hospital perfect he intends to hire "the damned best man there is to run it " (233). When Jack asks who this is, Willie answers, "Dr. Adam Stanton" (234). Stunned, Jack thinks the Boss has lost his mind. Jack's reaction here, similar to the one he had when Anne told him she had met with Willie for lunch, is based on his inability to see any connection between the high-minded and noble world of the Old South Stantons and the gritty, seamy arena of the Boss's New South politics. Because Jack has severed his allegiance to the Old South, two factors make him troubled by the Boss's decision to place his golden dream in the hands of the finest representative of that old world: He is fearful that the Boss will contaminate Adam, and he is distressed at the Boss's recognition of excellence in the old order, pragmatic though it may be.

But when the Boss said, "Get Stanton," he meant it, and so the next day finds Jack in Adam's run-down apartment with the offer "Governor Stark wants you to be director of the new hospital and medical center" (234–35). As expected, Adam refuses, but when Jack points out how much good Adam could do, he is almost persuaded to take the job. Nevertheless, Adam, the dutiful son of the good Governor Stanton, cannot bring himself to help with a project that would bring him into association with a man he believes is corrupt—certainly not one to be compared with his governor-father. While Jack no doubt agrees with Adam's assessment, it does not stop him from carrying out the Boss's wishes, since ultimately Jack and Willie want to achieve the same goal.

ANNE'S REQUEST

To Jack's surprise and mild disappointment he soon discovers he has an ally in his project to "Get Stanton" in the unlikely person of Anne. On a long, late-night walk Anne implores Jack to convince Adam to take the job as director. As they talk and walk along the docks by the river, several points become clear. Anne is nearly frantic about her brother's increasing submersion of himself in his work. Afraid that something drastic will happen and that she will lose him completely unless something is done to make him lead a more normal life, she believes that the directorship will give Adam the opportunity to break from his obsession with surgery. Jack, who is so good at explaining the psychological makeup of others, tells Anne that Adam's devotion to the cause of helping humankind is the product of a romantic temperament that has set impossibly high standards to live by, standards Adam has derived from his belief in an ideal father, Governor Stanton. Jack's assessment of Adam could apply to the romantic notions of the entire Old South culture, concepts that Mark Twain in *Life on the Mississippi* claimed were responsible for the Civil War. Because Adam has such an elevated vision of himself and the world, the only way to persuade him to act differently would be to change his concept of reality, since it would be ridiculous to try to change the nature of the world. Interestingly enough, Jack's clever and accurate evaluation of Adam would go a long way toward helping him understand his own problems—if only he had the power to listen to himself.

When Anne insists that Jack help her to save Adam from himself, Jack finally gives in and admits that perhaps he can help her, but a spark from his conscience keeps him from revealing what he has discovered from Miss Lily Mae Littlepaugh. Although Jack knows he should tell Anne what he has discovered, he can no longer resist her pitiful pleading and finally declares that he can turn Adam around by giving him a "history lesson" (248). Jack then reveals to Anne the Judge Irwin bribery affair, information that startles her but leaves her puzzled until it slowly dawns on her that her father, the noble Governor Stanton, was somehow involved. She is shocked and does not want to believe Jack, who did not want to hurt her with the information but nevertheless derives some pleasure at shattering her illusions about her father—another example of Jack's subconscious desire to destroy all in the old generation. "I have documents," Jack tells her before she catches a taxi and angrily leaves him (249). Five days later she telephones Jack and asks for the proof, "the photostat and the affidavit" from Miss Littlepaugh (252). The revelation in turn devastates Adam. When Anne urges him not to forfeit his love for their father, Adam replies, "Damn his soul to hell!" and immediately accepts the directorship of Willie's memorial hospital (253). Jack's search for the truth, which he thought could not harm anyone, has just destroyed the cherished ideal of his best friend.

ADAM AND THE BOSS

In the earlier clash between the forces of the Old and the New South, when Willie challenged Judge Irwin over his political support, the two opposing worldviews separated intact. But in this confrontation the leader of the New vanquishes a spokesperson for the Old, one whose heart has already been cut out by a New South henchman.

"Governor Stark, this is Dr. Stanton," Jack says, as he introduces his boss to the "Friend of His Youth" in Adam's apartment, where Willie has gone to confirm the offer of the hospital directorship (255). This section of the chapter begins as a dialogue between a hostile Adam and a friendly Willie but soon turns into a near monologue, with Willie lecturing Adam about his philosophy on life and politics. Along with the earlier explanation to Hugh Miller about the nature of law and human progress in chapter 3, it forms the core of Willie's pragmatic brand of New South politics. Willie believes that human beings invent concepts of good as it evolves and that good can come only from bad because "there isn't anything else to make it out of" (257). Willie's views on the evolution of humankind and the role of politics in that development stand in opposition to the social and political views of the traditionalists, who place their faith in what they consider to be unchanging verities. And in this scene at least, the reader may conclude that Willie has the stronger argument. Yet even though he has had his idealism badly shaken by the news about his father, Adam still does not like Willie or his rationale about the nature of the world. Nevertheless, he agrees to do the job if the governor will stay out of his way. Willie leaves the apartment, satisfied that he has the best person in the country to run his hospital. The New South can register one more victory over the Old.

That Willie has become a pragmatist who believes that the ends justify the means can be seen throughout the novel, especially in his dealings with Byram White, Judge Irwin, and Adam Stanton. Regarding the rule of law and his protection of White, he tells Hugh Miller, "Hell, the law is like the pants you bought last year for a growing boy, but it is always this year and the seams are popped and the shankbone's to the breeze. The law is always too short and too tight for growing humankind" (136). To Jack he reveals the underlying principle of his political philosophy when he orders him to dig up some wrongdoing in the judge's past: "Man is conceived in sin and born in corruption and he passeth from the stink of the didie to the stench of the shroud. There is always something" (49). Willie's pragmatic attitude toward the law and his warped, Calvinistic view of human nature free him to do anything in his power to improve the condition of the people in the state, even if he has to break the law to do so. When Willie visits Adam, he justifies his belief that all values are relative and constantly changing to suit the needs of the people. If the people want anything good out of life, they have to invent their notion of the good, and if they want to create good, the only place to get it is out of the bad in the world. As he told Hugh Miller, "You can't make bricks without straw, and most of the time all the straw you got is secondhand straw from the cowpen" (137).

With this harsh view of reality, Cousin Willie has become the Boss who can justify bribery, blackmail, and graft as long as they enable him to get the job done. He is an advocate of the people doing their will, a person of action who sees to it that highways, schools, and hospitals are built for his constituency. Yet as he gains more power to help the plain people, he begins to use that power to satisfy his own needs, just as his Old South predecessors had done, and one of those needs is to build a hospital with new bricks—bricks made from clean, fresh straw, a monument with no stain of corruption, as a memorial to the good part of the Willie who had believed in lofty ideals. Before too long, however, he is caught in a web of his own making. Believing he is above the law, he alienates his wife, Lucy; assuming he can direct his son's athletic career, he pressures the coach into letting the boy play; and he asks Jack for damaging information on Judge Irwin. The forces set in motion by Willie's self-interest can lead only to disaster.

Jack's Questions, Anne's Answer

Chapter 6 starts to wind down with Jack reflecting about the preceding events. He wonders why Willie Stark, who believes good can come from bad, has now become unyielding in his determination to keep the hospital free from the taint of politics. Why does he want to keep Tiny and Gummy away from the construction bids? This line of thinking reminds Jack of another question he once asked Willie, after his speech to the crowd gathered at the capitol to hear the outcome of the impeachment proceedings. Jack had asked Willie whether or not he meant it when he told the mob that his "strength was their will" and his "justice was their need" (262). Try as he might, Jack cannot come up with a solution to either of these riddles in Willie's personality, mainly because he cannot see that his own strength is founded on Willie's needs.

The third question that keeps nagging at Jack is, "How had Anne Stanton known about the hospital offer?" (263). How had she known to go to Adam's apartment to convince him to accept Willie's offer, since Jack had never mentioned it to her and is certain no one on Willie's staff could have told her? The question keeps rolling over and over in Jack's mind, until one day he finds the answer—one he does not want to hear.

Dr. Stanton and the Willie Stark Hospital

While sitting in his office one beautiful May morning, Jack is startled by the abrupt entry of Sadie, who is in a rage over Willie's latest sexual conquest. When he calms her down enough, he finds out the identity of the "high-toned" woman with whom the Boss is having an affair: It is none other than "Anne Stanton" (268). The message numbs Jack to the core of his being. He leaves the office and walks in a daze to Anne's apartment. When he looks at Anne, "she slowly nodded" (269). Jack has had his last question answered without speaking a word. Whoever Jack was before visiting Anne begins to undergo a radical change when he walks away from her apartment with the knowledge that she has gone to bed with Willie Stark. Jack's southern belle has tumbled from her pedestal.

Chapter 6 marks the turning point in the novel. Three of the characters have suffered shocks to their psyches, shocks they will have to learn to deal with. Anne and Adam have had their conception of their father destroyed, and Jack has had his ideal of Anne wrecked. Because Jack was so determined to carry out his mission to find out the scandal in the judge's background, he has uncovered knowledge that severely weakened the Stantons' proud idealism. It has led Adam to take the position of hospital director, and, Jack eventually learns, it has caused Anne to lower her moral standards and become Willie's mistress (even though it is not clear when the affair began). And Jack has had that one remaining fragment of goodness in his life shattered. The decisions made and the knowledge gained in this chapter will lead inexorably to the tragic events in the forthcoming chapters. This chapter has paved the way for further developments in Tom Stark's young life, in the relationship between Willie and Adam, in the Judge Irwin scandal, in the hospital contract, and, most important for the narrator, in Jack's love for Anne Stanton—a subject addressed in full in chapter 7.

11

Jack's Trip to the West

Before the events depicted in chapter 6 occur Jack Burden thought of himself as a free man, a modern individual who believes that the past has no discernible influence on one's life in the present and that the future will take care of itself. Once Jack learns about Anne's affair with Willie, however, his emotional life begins to undergo an upheaval that will change him drastically—and in important ways for the better, once he acknowledges his own personal past and his responsibility for the suffering he has caused others. The past does indeed live in Jack's present, and it will be his task to filter the good from the bad of the past generation if he is to live purposefully in the New South.

Chapter 7 shows Jack driving his automobile from the state capital (Baton Rouge, Louisiana) to Long Beach, California, and back again. Structurally it resembles chapter 1 with its road trip and chapter 4 because it contains a framed story. In this instance, however, the reader has no doubt at all about its relevance to the main narrative concerning Willie Stark and Jack Burden. Jack's trip out West and his return enclose the story of his love affair with Anne Stanton and his marriage to Lois Seager. And while this story does not advance the main plot, it greatly increases the reader's understanding of the lonely personal journey of Jack Burden. In effect it forms a large part of his spiritual autobiography.

HEADING WEST

When the world proves too much for Jack, he finds a way out, usually through a Great Sleep. In this case, though, the news about Anne and Willie sends him speeding at 75 miles an hour down a long narrow highway into the West—for the West is where a person goes when all else has failed. To Jack it is first an escape but later a place to start over again, just as it became in America's national myth of the Westward Expansion. When he gets behind the wheel of his car to start his journey, he is simply driving to get away from anything that reminds him of Anne and Willie and to put as many miles as he can between himself and the discovery that has shattered his life—somehow hoping that geographic distance will ease his pain. Racing across the country in his car, Jack allows his mind to travel a highway of his own into the memories of his past. The sound of the engine and the motion of the car lull him into dreaming "gently back over the years" (272).

Through a series of memory flashes from his childhood and early youth, he remembers Ellis Burden, his mother, Judge Irwin, the Count, the Young Executive, and Adam—all a part of the Old South culture that remains in his mind. Most of all, he remembers an awkward little girl who tagged along with him and Adam on their playful outings during their happy adolescence: Anne Stanton, the girl Jack loved long before he even knew it himself—and long after he thought their love was dead.

ANNE STANTON AT SEVENTEEN

Throughout most of this reminiscence, the reader sees Jack as genuinely happy for the first time. It is a far different mental state than he has been in for most of his adult life. As his memories restore the

Anne he fell in love with, Jack creates many lyrical passages in praise of the miracle in his life that was Anne. Together these prose passages represent one of the finest examples of the pastoral in modern fiction, but above all they illustrate the enduring power of the Old South myth of the belle, the lovely lady of perfection.

Jack's idyll begins during the summer of his twenty-first year when he returns to Burden's Landing from the state university. Anne was 17 and home on vacation from a finishing school in Boston. As Jack says, "And it was not like any summer which ever had been or was to be again" (273). At first Jack and Adam conduct their leisure activities with Anne as the tagalong third party, until one night Jack finds himself parked alone with Anne on a point overlooking the bay. Anne lays her head back against the seat with the moonlight on her face, and Jack is astonished at the wonder of her presence, much as Cass had been at Annabelle's in the Cass Mastern story. When Jack tries to speak, Anne lifts a finger to her lips and says, "Sh, sh!" and silences him with a knowing smile (275).

Like the vision he had of Anne floating on her back in the Gulf, the memory of this night will live in Jack's heart forever. Later that night while lying in bed, he bolts upright with the amazing insight that he is in love. He can scarcely believe the joy of this revelation. Similar to male characters in countless southern lyrics and novels, Jack has chosen to regard his love, Anne, as the epitome of southern womanhood. She is a child of beauty, a figure of pure delight, and a symbol of the highest spiritual values in Jack's soul. Although not initially obvious, this admiration of women has a negative side. When the belle is accorded such high esteem, she eventually becomes an unattainable ideal—and, unfortunately, removed from normal human experience. The beautiful, spiritualized heroine must always play the role of the perfect woman, for to behave in an ordinary way that would betray her humanity would deeply disturb her male admirers.

Jack is not only a product of the antebellum southern generation but also a person with an immediate personal past, one that has wounded him in a way he has not begun to understand as a man in love with his ideal. His love, though, is a bright woman with human passions and an active intellect despite the passive role of the belle that

Jack has imposed on her, and she has begun to sense that not all is right with Jack.

During the summer weeks Jack and Anne spend their evenings together; they kiss and tell each other "I love you"; and they drift along in their tender happiness until, near the end of the summer, Anne asks Jack what he plans to do with his life. Jack has never given the subject any thought, and he tells Anne he imagines he will go to law school. Anne, however, is not fooled; she knows he only thought up the idea on the spur of the moment, to satisfy her. Jack is puzzled by her serious concern about his answer, since he knows he can always come up with the money for their marriage and a job of some kind if she thinks he needs one. For some reason Anne considers this issue much more important than Jack does, and he just does not understand. Anne knows something Jack is unwilling to admit: His life has no sense of direction, because deep down he is an empty man, or, as Jack in the present says about himself at that time, "I had no ambitions" (285). This absence of purpose will slowly grow into a profound conflict between the young lovers. Neither Jack nor Anne can articulate that Jack's lack of a career goal indicates a deeper problem in his nature, some emptiness that prevents him from becoming a mature person willing to take on the responsibilities of an adult world. It does not matter to Anne what Jack does or how much money he makes, so long as he wants to do something. Through her intuition, this 17-year-old woman has discovered the great flaw in Jack's personality.

One other important event transpires during this fateful summer. On the night before Anne is to return to school in Boston Jack and Anne find themselves alone in the Burden mansion and decide to have sex for the first time. Jack's mother has called and said she and her friends would not be in until the early-morning hours. Jack and Anne slowly ascend the stairs to his bedroom in anticipation of the event that will seal their love for each other. Jack helps Anne undress, and she lies down on his bed. As Jack undresses, he looks at Anne lying nude before him, and he immediately "knew that everything was wrong, completely wrong" and is unable to touch her (295). Suddenly Jack hears his mother returning early to the house, and he rushes Anne to get dressed so that they will not be found together in an embarrassing situation. His mother and her friends have saved Jack from his moment of indecision with Anne.

Jack looks on his failure to proceed with their lovemaking as a big mistake in his life, and he is correct, but for reasons he does not completely understand. Jack's inability to make love to Anne no matter what the consequences is partly related to his uncertainty about what he wants to do with his life. Anne sees this correlation and so does the reader, but Jack will not make the connection until events in his life shake him free from his emotional debilitation. Also, Jack claims that had he not been "so noble" then, "everything would have been different," a phrase to be recalled later in the novel (297). The other reason he cannot touch Anne has to do with his heritage—a good southern gentleman does not violate the honor of his southern belle.

As a result of the skill of a gifted author, both the language and the situation in this part not only recall previous scenes but also prefigure scenes yet to come in the novel. First, Jack's claim that a sense of nobility prevented him from violating Anne reminds the reader of Cass Mastern's assertion that no one could claim any virtue until he or she had been enticed by an overpowering temptation. Second, the Cass Mastern–Annabelle Trice love affair with its wild fits of uncontrollable passion should be recalled here as a reminder of what Jack has relinquished with his refusal to make love to Anne. Third, Jack's declaration that things could have turned out differently forecasts the almost-identical statement Willie will make to Jack as Willie lies on his deathbed near the end of the novel.

After this summer the intensity of Jack and Anne's love diminishes, and Jack becomes increasingly discouraged about their relationship. He knows things are not going well, but he cannot figure out how to restore the magic of those wonderful few weeks when Anne was 17 and home on summer vacation. When he presses Anne to explain why she is turning away from him, she can only say, "It's because you are the way you are, Jackie" (299). While most of the blame for the disintegration of their love affair is Jack's, part of it too belongs to Anne, the daughter of a strong father who took good care of her and the product of a society that expected the wife to live in the reflected light of her husband's career. Anne is a proud person; she does not intend to marry a man who is going to be a psychological drifter, no matter how wealthy he may be. Like her father, her future husband must be a man of strength and purpose, someone perhaps more like Willie Stark than Jack Burden.

Jack then tries to attend law school on graduating from the state university but does so only because he had told Anne this was what he was going to do. He soon discovers that he hates it; instead of dropping out, however, he manages to get expelled. This feeble attempt at rebellion shows Jack as a passive-aggressive personality and proves Anne was right in her evaluation of him. When he gets involved in a small scandal with another woman, Jack and Anne go their separate ways. He becomes a reporter, starts reading history books, and eventually enters graduate school to study American history. He even marries a gorgeous, sexy woman named Lois Seager, though not because he loves her but because she is "juicy" (303). Lois had the misfortune to fall in love with a man who thinks of her only as a sex object. Beautiful, wealthy, and sociable, she would appear to be a good wife for the young Jack Burden, but the marriage is a mismatch from the beginning. Jack himself is puzzled about why Lois would marry a worthless person like him. And because his self-esteem is so low at this point in his life, he can only use Lois cynically to satisfy his sexual needs. Lois is not a sex machine, however; she is a real human being who sincerely loves Jack and only expects his love in return. For this she is destined to suffer Jack's cruelty and a failed marriage.

Jack's account of his marriage to Lois contrasts starkly to his previous descriptions of his love affair with Anne. As long as he can consider Lois a sex object, they get along fine, but once he starts to notice that she is more than a biological mechanism to satisfy his urges—once he starts to notice that she is a human being with thoughts and feelings of her own—Jack becomes destructive. At times even sadistic he does everything he can to disrupt their marriage. In a repetition of the way he got kicked out of law school Jack becomes passive in order to extricate himself from a bad situation instead of attacking the problem through direct action. The passages describing the tortured disintegration of his marriage to Lois show Jack at his worst, demeaning to himself and cruel to others. Finally, and mercifully this time, he enters one of his Great Sleeps and their marriage is over.

THE RETURN

Like Willie, his counterpart in the political realm, Jack develops a philosophical view of human nature that allows him to operate in the modern world with regard for neither the beliefs of an earlier generation nor any events from his own past. Lying on his hotel bed in Long Beach, Jack discovers what he believes to be a logical way to explain away all the unhappiness in his life. Words like *love* and *Anne Stanton* have no real meaning, and people act and react only in response to the biological workings of their glands and the mechanical twitchings of their nerves. His rationalization fills him with a new sense of confidence and releases him from the guilt and shame he feels over Anne and Willie's affair. He now returns to the capital with the belief that nothing can ever touch him again. But before ending this chapter Jack, the narrator in the present, lets the reader know that this stimulus-response philosophy he took such great comfort in eventually proved to be inadequate because it centers on the present and fails to accommodate the past and the future, just as it fails to integrate the body and the soul of the individual human being.

The structure of the different layers of time in this chapter supports the concept Jack's new philosophy tries to deny. From the perspective of the Jack who drove West, the time orientations of the chapter are past, present, and future. The past events happened from 1918 to 1920, the present is 1937, and the future is 1939—the perspective from which the narrator Jack is telling these events, which have now blended together into one organic whole.

12

Jack Burden's Father

The pace of the novel quickens dramatically in chapter 8 as the events rush to their tragic conclusion. Jack begins here confident in his new philosophy of human nature but ends by weeping over the death of his real father—Judge Montague Irwin. Jack's new philosophy attempts to remove notions of honor, fidelity, guilt, and responsibility from human emotional concern—all concepts that had once been part of the Old South's culture, as the Cass Mastern story had made clear. That a grown man would arrive at such a notion to absolve himself from any part he has played in the misery of those around him may be hard for the reader to accept unless he or she realizes just how desperate Jack is to give some order to a world that for him, at least, has become absurd. To Jack a mechanistic universe has at least some order and is not completely void of meaning, as his world became when his heroes and heroine lost their eminence. As the chapter progresses, Jack's behavior, though, grows more and more inconsistent with his new belief. He thinks of himself as a disinterested observer even as he becomes emotionally engaged in the lives of other people. Jack's humanity will not be denied, and in time he will learn how to salvage the best that a past generation has to offer—courage, love, and understanding.

THE GREAT TWITCH

Jack drives rapidly back to his home state from California, experiencing in his "secret knowledge" a "great strength" that has filled him with a renewed self-confidence (312). Driving through New Mexico, he stops at a filling station and talks to an old man who happens to have a facial tic. Noticing that the nerve disorder has nothing to do with the man's will or awareness, Jack seizes on the image as a way of generalizing about his theory of human nature, which he calls the "Great Twitch" (314). Variously labeled mechanism, behaviorism, determinism, positivism, or the stimulus-response philosophy, the Great Twitch releases its adherent from the necessity of accepting the consequences of free will. People who believe that human events are the result of random causes over which they have no control need not concern themselves with the emotional expense that attends human suffering. As Jack says, when you are "at one with the Great Twitch," you feel "clean and free" (314).

Back in the capital, Jack feels secure with his new knowledge and conducts his business for the Boss as usual, now more removed than ever from the ethics of his work. One evening while visiting Adam, he learns that his friend has scheduled a "prefrontal lobectomy" on a patient suffering from "catatonic schizophrenia" (316). Jack asks to attend the surgery as an interested reporter, since he has already witnessed an electrocution and three hangings. Adam grants his request, and the next day Jack watches intently as Adam uses his surgical tools to alter a human being's personality by removing portions of the patient's brain tissue. With just a few incisions and a couple of excavations, Adam succeeds in changing a moaning catatonic into a friendly extrovert. Jack looks on the operation, with its physical alteration of a human being's personality, as an exercise in mechanics and carpentry and considers it overall a fine illustration of the Great Twitch philosophy.

THE HUBERT COFFEE BRIBE

This section involves the complications of an attempted bribe of Adam, about half of which Jack reports as told to him by Anne, indicating they have reestablished communication during her affair with Willie. Further, as Jack tries to mend the damage caused by the bribery offer, his primary motivations are to help and protect Anne. Try as he might to look on Anne as merely an acquaintance, he cannot help but love her still. His own past slowly begins to reassert itself.

One night as Anne and Adam prepare dinner in Adam's old apartment, a sleazy character named Hubert Coffee turns up and tries to persuade Adam to throw the hospital contract to Gummy Larson. Adam punches Hubert in the mouth, an action that leaves him incredulous until he regains his composure and writes a letter of resignation to Willie Stark. Adam has mistakenly assumed that Willie sent Hubert on the errand.

Later Anne and Jack, at an all-night drugstore, discuss ways to convince Adam to remain as director. Jack comes up with a scheme to get the Boss to arrest Coffee on bribery charges and possibly topple Larson and MacMurfee in the bargain—if Anne will testify as a witness. Jack's mind races ahead to what would happen to Anne on the witness stand, and he recoils from his own plan because he suddenly realizes that Anne's affair with the Boss will be exposed. Overcome by emotion, Jack holds Anne's hands and asks, "Oh, Anne, why did you do it?" to which she replies, "He wasn't like anybody else" (325). She then reveals that Willie plans to divorce Lucy and marry her once he is elected to the U.S. Senate, a career move that is news to Jack. She further tells Jack that she saw no reason not to become involved with Willie once Jack had told her about her father's part in the Irwin scandal. Jack now meditates once more on the consequences of what he has done and what he has failed to do. He is at last beginning to consider his actions in the way that Cass Mastern finally came to see his as they impinged on the lives of other people. Back at Adam's apartment Jack convinces Adam that the Boss had nothing to do with the bribe, and Jack tears up the resignation letter.

TOM'S PATERNITY CASE

The summer continues in relative calm, except for an occasional screaming match between the Boss and Sadie over his active love life, until one day a seedy barber named Marvin Frey turns up in the Boss's office with the news that his daughter Sibyl is pregnant and Tom Stark is the expectant father, or, as it turns out, at least one of several prospects. The Boss becomes angry and throws Frey out. Yet he knows that the situation has the potential to lead to a damaging scandal that could wreck his forthcoming senatorial bid if MacMurfee gets wind of it—which he quickly does. While the Boss deals with the unwanted pregnancy as a nuisance and a matter of politics, his wife, Lucy, sees in it a baby that no one wants. When Jack visits Lucy to explain the sordid business to her, he reveals a deep concern for Lucy's feelings, just as he had done earlier with Anne's. Jack is genuinely touched by Lucy's goodness, her continuing devotion to Willie and Tom, and her tender concern for the unborn child. Somehow Jack's Great Twitch philosophy does not quite cover Lucy's love for Willie and her son, and neither does it completely explain Jack's awakening to the needs of others.

JUDGE IRWIN'S SUICIDE

In the final developments of the conflict between the political forces of the Old and the New South the Boss and Judge Irwin test the limits of their worldviews. And while the spokesperson for the old regime is physically vanquished by the modern South's new politician, his spirit will endure in the lives of Jack and his mother. Ironically, in the next chapter when Willie is destroyed, the best of his spirit will also prevail.

To halt the political scandal that would follow a paternity suit against Tom, the Boss tries to contact Marvin Frey and his daughter but learns that they have been sent out of state to protect them from his wiles until the day comes when MacMurfee can use them in his favor. Stymied, the Boss thinks up another possibility to halt MacMurfee in the senatorial race: getting Judge Irwin to step in and apply pressure against MacMurfee. Willie asks Jack if he has found out anything about Irwin that would force him to do his bidding. Jack replies that he has, but he has promised two people not to reveal it until he has presented his findings to the judge. He does not tell the Boss that the two people whose promise he is keeping are himself and Anne.

Back at Burden's Landing Jack cannot help but think of the happy times he once had with Anne. When he stops at his old home and learns from his mother that Irwin is ill, he fails to heed her admonition to leave the judge alone. Jack relentlessly continues his mission to confront the judge as his own ambivalence grows. At Irwin's he is greeted warmly by the judge, who is genuinely happy to see him, even given the previous harsh words between them about Willie Stark. Jack looks at the old man and feels a deep sense of affection for him as he thinks, "With all my heart, I discovered, I didn't want it to be true" (342). Against his feelings, Jack shows the judge the material he has dug up about the Littlepaugh suicide and the power company bribery. Deeply hurt, the judge admits his guilt but refuses to capitulate to the blackmail threat. When Jack tells the judge that he then has no option but to give the material to the Boss, the judge says enigmatically that he could stop Jack with a word, but he will not. Puzzled, Jack leaves the judge with his dignity intact. The judge's lifetime allegiance to the duties of the southern gentleman has left him with both a deep sense of honor and an abiding courage.

During the middle of the night Jack is awakened by his mother's high-pitched screams. Rushing to her room, he sees she has just dropped the telephone, whereupon she begins crying in anguish, "You killed him!" (349). Judge Irwin has shot himself in the heart. Mrs. Burden becomes hysterical and Jack has some difficulty figuring out what she means until she calms down enough to say, "Your father, . . . your father and oh! you killed him" (349). Before a doctor gives her a sedative she tells Jack that the judge was the only man she had ever loved. While his mother sleeps, Jack holds her hand and it dawns on him that he pities her but loves her too, "because she had loved somebody"

(352). From the depths of his past, Jack has at last learned about the reality of love in his family.

Mrs. Burden suffered many years of unhappiness because she fell in love with a man at the wrong time. When she came out of Arkansas as an attractive young woman with "famished" cheeks, she entered the elegant home of Ellis Burden as his wife, but she fell in love with Monty Irwin, a neighbor with an invalid wife. Because the judge was too honorable to leave his wife, Mrs. Burden endured a series of husbands she did not love on the mistaken assumption that she needed to provide her son with a substitute father. Since she and the judge could never unravel their tangled affair, Mrs. Burden remained confused about the depth of her love for the judge until he took his own life. Sadly, it was only at this point that she realized she had been living a lie. But her admission of the truth of their love offers her some consolation, while at the same time it gives their son, Jack, pride in his true identity.

Two days later the judge is buried, and Jack wonders about the connections between the Littlepaugh and Irwin suicides and the part he has played in the drama. He is relieved to know that Ellis Burden, the Scholarly-Attorney-turned-slum-preacher, is not his real father, because Jack has always considered him a weak man; however, Jack is no longer totally convinced of this view. He knows for certain, though, that he is proud of Judge Irwin, who had the strength to stand up to the threat of blackmail and not stop the scheme by telling Jack he was his real father. The next day Jack receives a call from the judge's executor, informing him that he is the sole heir to the dead man's estate. The irony of now owning what his father had salvaged through his one dishonest act strikes Jack as a bizarre joke, and he laughs hysterically until he finds himself crying in deep grief. To Jack the flow of tears "was like the ice breaking up after a long winter"(354). The internal connections between himself and his past have now been made, and Jack can begin the long-overdue process of healing.

Thus, chapter 8 ends paradoxically. On the one hand, Jack is grief-stricken over the loss of his biological father, a man who loved him and whom Jack loved in return. On the other hand, Jack has gained vital knowledge that was necessary for him to cast off the old, cynical, detached part of his personality, one he can now replace with a healthy, responsible emotional life. Stripped of illusions and phony rationalizations, Jack is now free to enter into a mature emotional life, one in which love, forgiveness, and compassion are not just empty words but livable realities, even if they are from the old generation's worldview. His mother's scream made it possible for Jack to be reborn, and this time with a complete psyche. The emotional involvement that will not be denied and the knowledge that suffering is a necessary part of the human experience are the twin midwives that were essential for Jack's spiritual rebirth.

13

The Assassination of Willie Stark

Jack remains an objective reporter throughout most of chapter 9, as he withdraws to mourn his losses, consider the world anew, and gather strength to make a new beginning. Although much of his personal story remains to be told, it is appropriate at this point in the narrative that he move into the background, since the events in the life of Willie Stark return dramatically to center stage for one last time. In this chapter the reader watches events through the mind of a narrator who has become aware of the interconnectedness of human lives. Jack makes it clear throughout this chapter that actions from the past weigh heavily on the events of the present and these in turn directly influence the future. He has become a modern-day Cass Mastern.

As Jack learns to accept the connection between past events and the present, he is at the same time slowly becoming responsible for his life and for those he loves. He is not, however, alone in his efforts at rehabilitation. His spiritual brother, Willie Stark, also begins his own attempt to restructure his life, and just as Jack begins to make amends with the Old South culture he has rejected, so Willie starts to make his peace with the plain folk, the ones whose love and respect endowed him with his initial success.

JACK'S RETREAT

Jack returns to the capital from the funeral at Burden's Landing, thinking that the Judge Irwin story is over. But as Jack the narrator remarks, "no story is ever over," and Jack realizes that, while he may have forgotten it temporarily, the Irwin matter is not closed, since it has a direct bearing on the Willie Stark story. One immediate result of the judge's death is that Jack refuses to figure out another angle to entrap MacMurfee or to bribe Marvin Frey and Sibyl. He will no longer be a party to threats, blackmail, or bribery as he waits to restore his own sense of ethics and propriety. He goes about his research now in an honest way, by working on a pending tax bill that is scheduled to go before the legislature.

Willie continues to worry about the Frey business, since it will damage his political image, but he forgets it easily when he watches his son, the star quarterback, play football on Saturday afternoons. Tom's game-day heroics, however, are not matched by his undisciplined behavior on other days of the week. His missed practices outrage the coach, upset his father, and, like so many other events in this chapter, have terrible consequences.

THE GUMMY LARSON DEAL

Willie is now confronted with the first dilemma of his tenure as governor and boss of the New South's political machine. He must do something to nullify MacMurfee, the last bastion of the good old boys in the state. But what can Willie do now that the judge has taken his own life and the Freys are being held incommunicado by MacMurfee in a neighboring state? He either can capitulate and let MacMurfee take the Senate seat, or he can deal with Gummy Larson and get him to call off MacMurfee. Both choices disgust Willie. The time is ripe for him to run for the Senate, but a deal with Larson will pollute the hospital project and dishonor his pledge to keep at least one part of his administration free from corruption.

Willie finally resolves his problem by joining Larson, who, with the hospital contract in hand, will stifle MacMurfee. The deal so enrages Willie that he threatens to tear Gummy limb from limb if he even thinks about cheating on the construction of the hospital building. Jack tells Willie that Tom Stark contributed to this unpleasant arrangement, but Willie refuses to understand the connection and only responds, "He's just a boy" (364). Jack's recognition of this connection is another clear sign of his increasing maturity.

Tom's Football Injury

Tom's sexual activities with Sibyl Frey gave the MacMurfee crowd leverage against the Boss, who focused his attention on the judge, who committed suicide. Jack now begins to see life more and more as a series of cause-and-effect relationships like this one. The segment on Tom's injury functions as a case history that illustrates Jack's new awareness.

Tom Stark, whom Willie sees as a refined version of himself, is an excellent football player and he knows it. He is a natural athlete with "snake-hips and pile-driver knees" who performs gracefully on the field and carries himself with arrogance at all times (366). Ruggedly handsome with bronze skin and a square jaw, he possesses a cocky assurance that lets the world know just how special he is. Since he is so confident in his football prowess, and because he is the governor's son, Tom sees no reason to follow the training rules set for the other players at the state university.

In a Saturday game against Tech that is supposed to be a romp Tom plays brilliantly until he starts showing off for the home crowd. During one play, however, he is hit by a defensive player as a result of his lapse in training and does not get up. Tom is paralyzed from the neck down, and his chances for survival are slim. Willie and Lucy decide to follow Dr. Adam Stanton's recommendation for surgery in the faint hope that Tom's spinal cord has not been crushed but only has a bone compressing it. After the surgery, though, Adam informs

Willie and Lucy that Tom's spinal cord was crushed, and the news so stuns Willie that Lucy must guide him to the waiting car. They leave together in silence. And so it goes in the tragedy of Tom Stark, All American. Had his father not been so indulgent, Tom would not have been so arrogant. And had Tom been more disciplined, he would not have suffered a crushed spinal cord on the football field. Willie knows that he is as much to blame for his son's injury as the opposing player who hit the boy.

DEATH IN THE CAPITOL

Since the events in the final part of this chapter are complex as well as sensational, Jack sticks closely to the chronology as the action unfolds. He begins the unit by reminding the reader that the illogic of the events gave "the whole occasion the sense of a dreamlike unreality" (383). After everything is over he will put the pieces of the puzzle together to see if he can find an underlying pattern and a semblance of meaning. By now the reader is neither surprised nor puzzled when Jack says, "[R]eality is not a function of the event as event, but of the relationship of that event to past, and future, events" (384).

When Jack goes to his office in the capitol on the Monday following Tom's surgery, he finds Tiny and the Boys hanging around, waiting to console the Boss when he comes in. Looking solemn and tired but clear-eyed, the Boss eventually comes to his office and gets rid of everyone except Jack and Tiny. Staring firmly at Tiny, the Boss says, "There won't be any contract with Larson" and orders him to "unfix" the deal (386). Greatly upset, Tiny leaves the office to carry out the Boss's order. Jack asks him why he changed his mind, and Willie says without elaboration, "You got to start somewhere" (387). But before he can make more than a start events he has set in motion interfere with his attempts at restitution.

When Jack receives an urgent message from Anne asking him to come to her apartment immediately, he finds her distraught over a visit from Adam. Adam had come to her earlier in the day, after receiving a telephone call from a man who told him that the only reason he had been made the hospital director was because his sister was Willie's mistress. Enraged, Adam told Anne he would not be "paid pimp to his sister's whore," after which he shoved her to the floor and left (389). Anne is terrified over what Adam might do, and she begs Jack to find him and explain everything to him. Adam, she says, is all she has left now because Willie has told her earlier in the day that their affair is over and that he is going back to his wife.

Through no fault of her own, Anne became the symbol of the innocent southern belle who must play the role her society demands of the pure woman or pay the consequences when she acts like a normal human being. Idolized by her father, her brother, and her youthful lover, Anne represents the good in the lives of these men who placed her on a plane high above the level of ordinary life with its blemishes, grief, and evil. And for a time in her life she is the perfect southern woman with her allegiance to home and family. To her father she is so devoted that she becomes his nurse for the last seven years of his life and after his death a living memorial to his honorable name—thereby isolating herself even further from the fullness of life. Adam, the perfectionist brother and noble father's son, expects her to continue this role as the emblem of the Stanton family honor. His discovery that Anne is merely human drives him to homicide. Ironically, though, Anne is victimized most by Jack Burden. Although she loves him, she can see that Jack is a hollow man who cannot even have sex with her. To Jack Anne is the essence of southern virtue, and to touch her naked body would violate not only her sexual purity but also his ideal of her as the one perfect good in his life. When Anne becomes involved with a charismatic man of direction and power, a man who has no concept of the southern aristocrat's worship of women, she initiates a chain reaction that leads to the deaths of her lover as well her brother. By no means the sole cause of the tragedy, Anne suffers grief and guilt over her decision to stop playing the role of the southern belle, a role she had no choice but to accept—that is, until she met Willie Stark.

Unable to locate Adam, Jack meets Willie in the office. They move into the lobby under the capitol dome, and Jack spots Adam, his clothes soaked and muddy, standing next to a statue. Adam walks toward Willie, who extends his hand, and Jack thinks, *"He's shaking hands with him, he's all right now, he's all right"* (396). Just then he sees the small gun in Adam's hand and the two bursts of fire from the barrel. Another rapid series of gunshots from Sugar-Boy's weapon drops Adam, dead before he hits the floor.

Adam was once the perfect inheritor of the highest standards of the Old South. His idealistic beliefs, though, had already proved impossibly fair and strong. Yet after learning that Governor Stanton was not a god Adam still maintained a belief in himself, in his own ability to make a difference in an evil world. What Adam could not accept, however, was the notion that he had received the hospital directorship not on his own merits but through his perfect sister's whorish behavior. Learning that his father was inadequate had shaken his belief in his heritage, but the knowledge that he and his sister were inadequate delivers a blow to his psyche from which he never recovered. Driven insane by the false realization that he had been a pawn in a sexual game between his sister and the Boss, Adam destroyed the man he thinks was the one responsible for his diminished self.

Willie has suffered serious wounds but does not die immediately. At one time it appears that he might pull through; however, an infection develops and he fades rapidly. In his last few hours he sends for Jack, and on his deathbed he asks why Adam had shot him. But Jack says he does not know. Looking at Jack for the last time, Willie says, "It might have been different, Jack," and begs him to believe it (400). Willie dies the next morning.

In addition to Tom's injury and the deaths of Willie and Adam, Jack has mentioned in passing other matters, ones the reader will understand later as contributing factors in the final tragedy. Tiny Duffy had left the Boss's office frustrated over the cancellation of the Gummy Larson contract, knowing he would not get his kickback for a deal he believed he arranged. And Sadie Burke had become highly irritated over something the Boss told her, something the reader may assume is the same message he gave Anne—that he was going to give his marriage another chance. The links contributed by Tiny and Sadie to the chain of events that ended on the capitol floor will become clear in the next chapter.

Through Willie's own stubbornness and willful refusal to listen to his wife's urging him to change his ways, he was responsible for the devastating injury to his son. Yet instead of attempting to rationalize his part in Tom's accident, he accepted the responsibility for his actions and tried to reassert the good values from the early part of his career. By returning to Lucy and renouncing his mistresses he reaffirmed the sanctity of his marriage, and by ordering Tiny Duffy to undo the Larson deal he signaled his intention to reconstruct his political life. In effect he wanted to reject the bad and to develop the good in the New South that he had helped create. But too much had happened, too many people had been hurt, too many betrayals and dishonors had occurred to turn back the hands of time. Nevertheless, as Willie died, he was convinced that he had changed and that he could have made even more of a difference had he remained true to his early ideals.

Willie Stark is one of the great creations in American literature. Like Captain Ahab and Jay Gatsby, he fascinates the reader with his mixture of good and bad. On the one hand, Willie has heroic qualities; he has the ambition and talent to lead his state to a better life. A reader may even take some delight when Willie revenges himself on his enemies and perhaps secretly admire him as he gains more and more power. Just as Willie satisfies the "secret needs" of Sadie, Anne, Adam, and Jack, so he does with the reader. On the other hand, the reader is appalled by Willie's villainous qualities—his humiliation of his underlings, his bleak view of human nature, and his willingness to destroy the lives of others to accomplish his goals. If the reader is also a little embarrassed to see a part of Willie in his or her own personality, he or she can also be encouraged by Willie's late rebirth for the promise it holds for every flawed human being.

14

Resolution and a New Beginning

In chapter 10, the final chapter of *All the King's Men*, Jack pulls together the loose ends of the narrative and attains a new level of understanding that gives his life a fresh direction. To make sense out of the violent deaths of the judge, Willie, and Adam he must gather a few more facts that will prove unsettling and potentially destructive, and he will have to decide how to use that information in a responsible way. Jack then spends some time assimilating his new knowledge before he understands for the first time in his life what he meant when he claimed that knowledge is power. He confirms two lessons that have slowly been seeping into his awareness since the death of Judge Irwin. First, he learns that power, no matter how it is gained, can be used for good or ill, and that each individual is alone responsible for that choice. Second, he learns that each person must accept the past in order to live in the present and look forward to the future. While Jack does not undergo so dramatic a conversion as would send him out to a missionary field in the service of God as it had done Mr. Burden, he does commit himself to the belief that life is worth living despite its hardships and miseries. He has come to respect himself and to love others.

RETURN TO BURDEN'S LANDING

The chapter begins with a brief description of another automobile trip, this one with two cars—a hearse bearing Adam Stanton's body, followed by a black limousine with Anne—traveling to the cemetery at Burden's Landing. After Willie dies and is buried Jack also returns to Burden's Landing to be near Anne while they both recuperate from their grief. They take long walks and sit together on the gallery at the Stanton house, and except for Jack's reading a novel to Anne, they rarely talk to each other, having reached an unspoken understanding that being together in silence is what they need for the moment. To break their "conspiracy of silence" would mean they would have to admit that they were largely responsible for the deaths of Willie and Adam, and this they will do after time has eased their immediate grief (405). These quiet days remind Jack of the summer 20 years earlier, when he fell in love with Anne.

Jack's mind drifts slowly back over the events of the preceding few weeks and eventually focuses on an issue that will not go away: Who told Adam about Willie and Anne? When the question continues to nag him, he forces himself to ask Anne if she knows the answer, but all she is sure of is that the telephone call had come from a man. Not content to let the matter drop, Jack leaves Burden's Landing to find out if Sadie Burke might help him find the answer.

SADIE'S ANSWER

Returning to the capital, Jack discovers that Sadie has left the city. But he eventually tracks her down in the Millett Sanatorium, where she has admitted herself for exhaustion. Sadie does not want to talk to Jack, and he notices that her eyes, her only beautiful feature, have lost their fire. Despite her reluctance, Jack persists in questioning her about the identity of the caller who sent Adam into a murderous rage, and she finally tells him it was Tiny Duffy. All is now clear to Jack, and since Sadie never wants to go back to the capital, Jack himself will have to decide how to use the knowledge of Tiny's involvement, information that fills Jack with "a great joy and relief" (411).

GOVERNOR TINY DUFFY

Tiny Duffy, who had been lieutenant governor when the Boss was alive, is now the governor of the state. When Tiny asks Jack to come see him, Jack goes immediately. At the Governor's Mansion Jack finds Tiny posturing in the role of the big-time politician. With Willie gone, Tiny thinks it will be business as usual in state politics, and he offers to retain Jack in his old "research" position. Furious, Jack calls him "the stinkingest louse God ever let live" and then accuses him of killing the Boss (414). In his outburst Jack admits to Tiny that his phone call to Adam at least indicated he was a human being with enough spirit to be capable of revenge, which fact surprised Jack, since he had always thought of Tiny as a coward. Jack stalks out of the governor's office "feeling like a million and thinking of himself as a hero" (415). A few hours later, though, his exhilaration turns to bitterness as it dawns on him that Tiny had offered him the job only because he thought of Jack as a coconspirator. Jack thinks, "It was as though in the midst of the scene Tiny Duffy had slowly and like a brother winked at me" (417). Tiny is right, of course, and Jack knows now that the people he has come to hate are just like himself. For the first time in his life Jack understands that he is vitally connected with his flawed fellow human being.

THE JOKE ON SUGAR-BOY

The realization of his kinship with people like Tiny sends Jack into another one of his periods of withdrawal, but at least this time he does not go into one of his Great Sleeps. He stays away from people he knows, even Anne; sits in bars; goes to the movies; and spends hours in the public library. It is here one day that he runs into Sugar-

Boy O'Sheean, ex-bodyguard and ex-driver. As they talk about old times, Jack sees in a flash of inspiration how he can get rid of Tiny Duffy. He leads Sugar-Boy to consider what he would do if he found out that Adam Stanton had been framed, that someone else had put Adam up to killing the Boss. Jack hears the answer he expected— Sugar-Boy would "kill the son-of-a-bitch"—but just as he starts to give Sugar-Boy the name, he sees in his mind's eye the face of Tiny winking at him "like a brother" (420). Having brought Sugar-Boy to a frantic state, Jack knows his own life is in danger. Instead of giving him the information that would kill Tiny and Sugar-Boy too, however, Jack says, "I was kidding," and thinks for a moment he is a "goner" (421). Sugar-Boy calms down, though, and Jack leaves him, doing so with some regrets because he realizes he has denied Sugar-Boy a chance to fulfill his purpose in life—as deadly as it may be. Jack's newfound knowledge of his shared humanity has given him a deep sense of responsibility that he previously lacked. His refusal to divulge to Sugar-Boy the deadly information is a certain mark of his entry into a responsible adult life.

Lucy's Grandchild

In the spring Jack feels that a change has come over him in the way he views the world, and one of the things he is now prepared to do is to pay Lucy Stark a visit. In the parlor of the farmhouse where she is living he and Lucy discuss Tom's death from pneumonia a month earlier. Lucy then takes Jack into a backroom and shows him a baby in a crib. She claims it is Tom's baby, and while Jack is somewhat doubtful, Lucy is committed to believing that Tom was the father. She paid Sibyl Frey $6,000 to let her adopt the child, whom she has named Willie Stark because she has come to believe that "Willie was a great man" (426). As Jack leaves the farm, he thinks that he too must believe that Willie was a great man. Although the realization does not free him from his guilt in the deaths of Willie, the judge, and Adam, it does permit him to "think better of all other people," including himself (427).

By accepting responsibility for his words and deeds Jack has become reconciled to the past.

A Son's Gift

In early summer Jack goes back to Burden's Landing, where his mother tells him she is leaving Theodore, the Young Executive, and giving him her beautiful house. Jack is surprised at her decision, but as they talk she tells him again that Judge Irwin was the only man she had ever loved, a fact she has only recently admitted. The next day, as Jack and his mother wait for the train that will take her to Reno for the divorce, she asks him what he and the judge had talked about the day Irwin killed himself. Jack tells her that although they had a minor argument over politics, the judge had primarily complained about his failing health. This lie is his mother's "going-away present" (432). Greatly relieved that it was not because of something Jack said that the judge killed himself, Jack's mother now leaves with peace of mind. Jack has been deceptive but also honorable and responsible in his reply to his mother.

A Mother's Gift

While Jack gave his mother a gift of love by covering up the truth, he received an equally valuable one from her when she revealed the truth. By showing her deep love for the judge she gave Jack a "new picture of the world," and now he can accept his past, which before had disgusted him (432). At peace with himself for the first time he feels confident that he can pick up the fragments of his life and move on. The first thing he does is visit Anne and tell her the complete story of Judge Irwin and his mother.

Jack concludes his story of Willie Stark, which, as he said, is his own story, in 1939, the present perspective from which all of the preceding events have been told. In a few quick sketches he lets the reader know that he has moved into the judge's house with Anne, his new wife, and that they have brought the ailing Ellis Burden home to live with them. At present he has returned to writing the book on the life of Cass Mastern, and he intends to go to work for Hugh Miller, the honest attorney general, when Miller decides to reenter politics.

Jack Burden at last becomes a free man who has learned to accept the past and to live in the present as a responsible human being. He has learned that although the Old South's culture was flawed, it should not be completely discarded, for it also stood for the substantial values of family, devotion to duty, and honorable public service— all virtues Jack can now believe will find their place in the New South.

Afterword: Jack Burden—From Cynicism to Acceptance

All the King's Men is an unusual novel in that it has two dynamic characters; that is, characters whose personalities undergo significant change as the events of the narrative unfold. These two characters are Willie Stark and Jack Burden, one a person of action and the other a detached observer. The fact that both men develop throughout the novel has led to a debate among critics as to which one is the more important character. While this issue may initially strike the reader as trivial, an examination of the problem can help the reader to see what *All the King's Men* finally contributes to the never-ending struggle to understand the basic truths of human nature.

If the reader selects Willie Stark as the central character, he or she will have chosen someone who excites the reader's interests in the role of the powerful leader in society. Willie illustrates the problems of the leader who accrues more power than any one person should have in a democracy. In the first three chapters and in two subsequent ones he is the most stimulating character in the novel, and certainly more interesting than Jack, because the reader sees him function in sensational ways that often startle through his audacity and strength of will. Further, Willie has the two prerequisites that a public figure in America needs to ascend to the highest levels of the political realm— words and deeds. America's most enduring heroes must "say" and "do." Abraham Lincoln saved the Union and delivered an unforgettable address at Gettysburg. Franklin D. Roosevelt led the country out of the Great Depression as he spoke nobly of "the only thing we have to fear is fear itself." Willie has both of these attributes, and the reader applauds him in his promising career. Yet as Willie becomes the Boss the reader witnesses the machinations of the politics of demagoguery and is reminded of the old axiom that power corrupts but absolute power corrupts absolutely. The reader watches with fascination the corruption of a good man who begins to use his enormous political power to satisfy his own needs. Above all, through the rise and fall of Willie Stark the reader learns what to expect in the modern state when political power loses its constructive purpose.

If the reader concludes that Jack Burden is the central character of *All the King's Men*, he or she will have selected someone whose problems in coming to terms with the world are ones that everyone can relate to. Like most readers, Jack wants to know "Who am I?" and "Is life worth living?" Jack's struggle to discover his identity and a sense of the forward motion in life is a universal one, and the resolution of his quest provides the reader with insights that may prove instructive in his or her own journey toward self-knowledge. In Jack the reader witnesses the consequences of intellect without direction and, more important, the renewal of self that is possible after great suffering and the acceptance of responsibility.

Every sentence, every thought, in *All the King's Men* comes to the reader through the mind of Jack Burden. Jack even chooses the portions of Cass Mastern's journals and letters for the reader's consideration. He is the one who documents the career of Willie Stark and makes him the center of the reader's attention. By reporting and commenting on Willie Jack brings him alive and gives the reader all he ever knows about Willie. Because he tells the reader all that goes on, Jack is the central developing consciousness in the narrative, no matter how much of the story is devoted to Cass Mastern and Willie Stark.

When the novel opens, Jack is the special research assistant to the most powerful man in the state. Intelligent and articulate, Jack combines a natural curiosity about people with skills he has developed as a history student and as a reporter to serve the Boss energetically in the pursuit of information to use against his political foes. The Boss, in answering some "secret need" in Jack, inspires him with a sense of purpose that engages him intellectually. Yet when the reader first sees Jack, he or she watches a man who, while doing his job very well, stands back and observes the action without any serious emotional commitment. For reasons not clear at first Jack has made a separate peace with his fellow human beings and has adopted an attitude of cynical indifference in order to function in a world that to him is essentially void of meaning.

Owing to childhood events that left him spiritually debilitated, Jack becomes a wisecracking smart aleck with a know-it-all sense of humor. His attitude, while often repulsive and insensitive, is one that Americans, especially younger generations, sympathize with and occasionally find attractive, even in their popular entertainers. Americans have always enjoyed mocking authority and poking fun at the rich and famous. "Wiseguy" humor satisfies Americans' need to tweak the noses of arrogant people and asserts a type of independence from centralized corrosive power. Jack's attitude was especially appealing to Americans after World War II, for they had witnessed the result of masses of people following a powerful leader. And it is more than a coincidence that during the 1950s, when *All the King's Men* was enjoying its widest readership, the most popular movies with American youth were *Rebel without a Cause*, *The Wild One*, and *Blackboard Jungle* (in which a "juvenile delinquent" calls his teacher Daddy-O).

Jack Burden is witty and insightful, but he is also sick in his soul. He whines too much, follows orders without question, and shuts himself off from others. His intellectual stance slowly begins to irk the reader the more it resembles shallow indifference and callousness toward those who really care for him. His use of such abstractions as "brassbound Idealism" and the "Great Twitch" aggravates the reader as only some clever theories used to justify villainy and to excuse him from social responsibility. Jack is not a whole person, and his incompleteness is seen in all his relationships. For instance, while he admires and likes Willie, he sees him for the corrupt person he is, yet he does not object to his actions and even aids him in the blackmail schemes by rationalizing that unearthing the truth about a person's life cannot be harmful to anyone. In his best smart-aleck manner he describes his research on the background of Judge Irwin as finding "the deceased fly among the raisins in the rice pudding" (192). Historical researchers in his line of business actually perform a valuable service by giving "definition" to the lives of those long gone; as he cynically remarks, all "historical researchers" believe as he does, "And we love truth" (228). Until he undergoes a rebirth, Jack is incapable of knowing the "truth" about human nature.

One part of Jack hates his mother and his reputed father, and he has closed out Anne from his life—all people who could have loved him unconditionally. Thus, throughout much of the novel Jack has denied the emotional centers of his personality. But because the story is told in retrospect, the reader knows that Jack has not been totally successful in ridding himself of all emotion. As Jack goes through the process of discovering those repressed feelings, the reader watches the miracle of rebirth and participates in a realistic triumph over spiritual inertia.

As an adult, Jack is limited emotionally because of circumstances in his childhood that affected him in ways that will take years to understand. Like the child of alcoholic parents or the victim of sexual abuse, Jack has little choice but to adopt a strategy for survival, in his case the self-protective camouflage of cynicism. His parents—Ellis Burden, Mrs. Burden, and Monty Irwin—had no idea that the way they conducted their lives would have repercussions in their son's emotional life that would be as influential to the development of his temperament as the genes from his biological parents would be on his physical development. When Ellis Burden walked away as Jack's father, he left the child with a mother ill-equipped to assist in a young boy's emotional growth. Because the truth of his parentage and his mother's love for his real father remain hidden, Jack creates destructive notions about his own identity. For most of his adult life Jack's emotional being remains sterile, largely because his memories are mainly accusatory ones. Instead of a rich fund of sustaining reminiscences from his past, Jack has only a few images of his fathers and Anne to give substance to his emotional existence. It is no wonder that he became a history student and is so good at imaginatively re-creating the inner lives of other people, since he is so lacking in a store of his own affirmative memories. It takes his mother's scream at the death of his real father to give birth to a new Jack Burden and force him to reevaluate who he is.

Jack is a gifted storyteller who entrances the reader; at the same time his passive behavior irritates. As Jack begins reconstructing his identity, however, his words and his actions start to coalesce, verifying his acceptance of himself and others as flawed human beings worthy of trust and understanding. Like Willie, Jack must also become good with words and deeds. And when his actions begin to match his words, the reader begins to rearrange his or her notions about Jack's character. Jack learns, among other things, that what people say and what they do are frequently at odds, but moral people will make the attempt to bring their words and deeds into a reasonable alignment.

Jack's story is one of movement. He travels a lonely road from the warmth and security of an innocent Old South childhood at Burden's Landing into the cynical New South world of the frustrated loner who wears a mask to hide the hurt from the past and to obscure the obligation that lies just around the next bend in the road. Jack's odyssey leads him through disasters into the heart of darkness, but his voyage, unlike Willie's, does not end there. Jack is granted permission to continue his trip and to return to his loved ones—ready now to accept the irony of existence and to enter "into the convulsion of the world, out of history into history and the awful responsibility of Time" (438). Jack Burden has put Jack Burden together again.

Notes and References

Chapter 1

1. T. Harry Williams, *Huey Long* (New York: Alfred A. Knopf, 1970), 4, 6.

2. Allan P. Sindler, *Huey Long's Louisiana* (Baltimore, Md.: Johns Hopkins University Press, 1956), 1; hereafter cited in text.

3. Robert Penn Warren, "Introduction," *All the King's Men* (New York: Random House, 1953), v; hereafter cited in text as "Intro."

Chapter 3

1. *"All the King's Men," Catholic World* 164 (November 1946): 189.

2. Harold C. Gardiner, "Why Put Him Together Again?" *America* 75 (24 August 1946): 503.

3. [W. K. R.], "Humpty Dumpty Had a Great Fall," *Christian Science Monitor*, 4 September 1946, 18.

4. Orville Prescott, "Outstanding Novels," *Yale Review* 36 (August 1946): 192.

5. Robert Davis, "Dr. Adam Stanton's Dilemma," *New York Times Book Review*, 18 August 1946, 3.

6. Diana Trilling, "Fiction in Review," *Nation* 163 (24 August 1946): 220.

7. George Mayberry, "On the Nature of Things," *New Republic* 115 (2 September 1946): 265.

8. J. P. Wood, "Mr. Warren's 'Modern Realism,'" *Saturday Review of Literature* 29 (17 August 1946): 11.

9. Granville Hicks, "Some American Novelists," *American Mercury* 63 (October 1946): 499.

10. Henry Rago, "Books of the Week," *Commonweal*, 4 October 1946, 599; hereafter cited in text.

11. Robert Penn Warren, "A Note to *All the King's Men*," *Sewanee Review* 61 (July–September 1953): 480.

Chapter 4

1. "Interview with Robert Penn Warren," in *The World's Hieroglyphic Beauty*, ed. Peter Stitt (Athens: University of Georgia Press, 1985), 253.

Selected Bibliography

Primary Sources

Novels

All the King's Men. New York: Harcourt, Brace, 1946.
At Heaven's Gate. New York: Harcourt, Brace, 1943.
Band of Angels. New York: Random House, 1955.
The Cave. New York: Random House, 1959.
Flood: A Romance of Our Time. New York: Random House, 1964.
Meet Me in the Green Glen. New York: Random House, 1971.
Night Rider. Boston: Houghton Mifflin, 1939.
A Place to Come To. New York: Random House, 1977.
Wilderness: A Tale of the Civil War. New York: Random House, 1961.
World Enough and Time: A Romantic Novel. New York: Random House, 1950.

Short Stories

The Circus in the Attic and Other Stories. New York: Harcourt, Brace, 1947.

Poetry

Audubon: A Vision. New York: Random House, 1969.
Being Here: Poetry 1977–1980. New York: Random House, 1980.

Brother to Dragons: A Tale in Verse and Voices. New York: Random House, 1953.

Chief Joseph of the Nez Perce. New York: Random House, 1983.

Eleven Poems on the Same Theme. Norfolk, Conn.: New Directions, 1942.

Incarnations: Poems 1966–1968. New York: Random House, 1968.

New and Selected Poems, 1923–1985. New York: Random House, 1985.

Now and Then: Poems 1976–1978. New York: Random House, 1978.

Or Else—Poem/Poems 1968–1974. New York: Random House, 1974.

Promises: Poems 1954–1956. New York: Random House, 1956.

Rumor Verified: Poems 1979–1980. New York: Random House, 1981.

Selected Poems: New and Old, 1923–1966. New York: Random House, 1966.

Selected Poems, 1923–1943. New York: Harcourt, Brace, 1944.

Selected Poems, 1923–1975. New York: Random House, 1976.

Thirty-six Poems. New York: Alcestis Press, 1935.

You, Emperors, and Others: Poems 1957–1960. New York: Random House, 1960.

Other Works

"*All the King's Men*: The Matrix of Experience." *Yale Review* 53 (Winter 1965): 161–67.

An Approach to Literature: A Collection of Prose and Verse with Analyses and Discussions, with Cleanth Brooks and John T. Purser. Baton Rouge: Louisiana State University, Department of English, 1936.

Democracy and Poetry. Cambridge, Mass.: Harvard University Press, 1975.

"Introduction." *All the King's Men*, v–x. New York: Random House, 1953. First published in *Sewanee Review* 61 (July–September 1953): 476–80.

John Brown: The Making of a Martyr. New York: Payson & Clark, 1929.

The Legacy of the Civil War: Meditations on the Centennial. New York, Random House, 1961.

Modern Rhetoric, with Cleanth Brooks. New York: Harcourt, Brace, 1949.

Portrait of a Father. Lexington: University Press of Kentucky, 1988.

The Rime of the Ancient Mariner. New York: Reynal & Hitchcock, 1946.

A Robert Penn Warren Reader. Edited by Albert Erskine. New York: Random House, 1987.

Robert Penn Warren Talking: Interviews 1950–1978. Edited by Floyd C. Watkins and John T. Hiers. New York: Random House, 1980.

Segregation: The Inner Conflict in the South. New York: Random House, 1956.

Selected Essays. New York: Random House, 1987.

Understanding Fiction, with Cleanth Brooks. New York: F. S. Crofts, 1943.

Understanding Poetry: An Anthology for College Students, with Cleanth Brooks. New York: Henry Holt, 1938.

Who Speaks for the Negro? New York: Random House, 1965.

Secondary Sources

Bibliographies

Grimshaw, James A. *Robert Penn Warren: A Descriptive Bibliography.* Charlottesvillle: University Press of Virginia, 1981.

Nakadate, Neil. *Robert Penn Warren: A Reference Guide.* Boston: G. K. Hall, 1977.

Books

"All the King's Men": A Symposium. Carnegie Series in English, no. 3. Pittsburgh, Pa.: Carnegie Press, 1957. Seven original essays on a variety of subjects.

Beebe, Maurice, and Leslie A. Field, eds. *Robert Penn Warren's "All the King's Men."* Belmont, Calif.: Wadsworth, 1966. Essays on Huey Long, literary sources, and several representative approaches to the novel.

Bohner, Charles. *Robert Penn Warren.* Boston: Twayne, 1964, rev. 1981. Good general introduction to Warren's life and literature.

Burt, John. *Robert Penn Warren and American Idealism.* New Haven, Conn.: Yale University Press, 1988. Interesting chapter on the "emergence" of the romantic temperament in a realistic novel.

Casper, Leonard. *Robert Penn Warren: The Dark and Bloody Ground.* Seattle.: University of Washington Press, 1960. First book-length study on Warren; emphasizes poetic development.

Chambers, Robert H., ed. *Twentieth Century Interpretations of "All the King's Men."* Englewood Cliffs, N.J.: Prentice-Hall, 1977. Excellent collection of solid essays.

Clark, William Bedford. *Critical Essays on Robert Penn Warren.* Boston: G. K. Hall, 1981. Substantial selections of representative reviews and critical essays spanning Warren's career from the mid-1940s to the late 1970s.

Gray, Richard. *The Literature of Memory: Modern Writers of the American South*. Baltimore, Md.: Johns Hopkins University Press, 1977. Warren as a southern author who explores the conflict between the actual and the ideal.

———, ed. *Robert Penn Warren: A Collection of Critical Essays*. Englewood Cliffs, N.J.: Prentice-Hall, 1980. Good collection that illustrates breadth of Warren's career.

Guttenburg, Barnett. *Web of Being: The Novels of Robert Penn Warren*. Nashville, Tenn.: Vanderbilt University Press, 1975. Examines the novels in terms of existentialist thought.

Justus, James H. *The Achievement of Robert Penn Warren*. Baton Rouge: Louisiana State University Press, 1981. First attempt to view Warren's poetry, fiction, and nonfiction prose as thematically related.

Longley, John Lewis, ed. *Robert Penn Warren: A Collection of Critical Essays*. Useful collection of 16 essays on themes, fiction, and poetry.

Sindler, Allan P. *Huey Long's Louisiana*. Baltimore, Md.: Johns Hopkins University Press, 1956. Traces causes of Longism and its influence on state politics.

Snipes, Katherine. *Robert Penn Warren*. New York: Frederick Ungar, 1983. Overview of Warren's long career with analysis of stages thereof.

Strandberg, Victor H. *The Poetic Vision of Robert Penn Warren*. Lexington: University Press of Kentucky, 1977. Solid study of Warren's poetry.

Williams, T. Harry. *Huey Long*. New York: Alfred A. Knopf, 1970. The definitive biography of the Kingfish.

Articles

Anderson, Charles R. "Violence and Order in the Novels of Robert Penn Warren." *Hopkins Review* 6 (Winter 1953): 88–105. Warren's first four novels begin with historical violence and move to a restoration of order through cultural tradition.

Cottrell, Beekman W. "Cass Mastern and the Awful Responsibility of Time." In *"All the King's Men": A Symposium*, 39–49. Pittsburgh, Pa.: Carnegie Press, 1957. The importance of the Mastern journals and the spiderweb theory to *All the King's Men*.

Girault, Norton R. "The Narrator's Mind as Symbol: An Analysis of *All the King's Men*." *Accent* 7 (Summer 1947): 220–34. Centers on Jack as protagonist and examines imagery of rebirth.

Heilman, Robert B. "Melpomeme as Wallflower; or, The Reading of Tragedy." *Sewanee Review* 55 (January–March 1947): 154–66. Pioneering discussion of *All the King's Men* as a modern novel that reconstructs classical and Renaissance tragedy.

Selected Bibliography

Katope, Christopher G. "Robert Penn Warren's *All the King's Men*: A Novel of Pure Imagination." *Texas Studies in Literature and Language* 12 (Fall 1970): 493–510. Examines sun and moon imagery as aid to characterization.

Kerr, Elizabeth M. "Polarity of Themes in *All the King's Men*." *Modern Fiction Studies* 6 (Spring 1960): 25–46. Excellent study of the conflict between action and thought in the narrative.

Meckier, Jerome. "Burden's Complaint: The Disintegrated Personality as Theme and Style in Robert Penn Warren's *All the King's Men*." *Studies in the Novel* 2 (Spring 1970):7–21. Helpful analysis of the theme of the divided self.

Mizener, Arthur. "Robert Penn Warren: *All the King's Men*." *Southern Review* 3 (Autumn 1967): 874–94. Superb overview of the novel, emphasizing characters' need to become engaged in public life.

Nakadate, Neil. "Robert Penn Warren and the Confessional Novel." *Genre* 2 (December 1969): 326–40. Sees confession as necessary path for Jack's redemption.

Payne, Ladell. "Willie Stark and Huey Long: Atmosphere, Myth, or Suggestion?" *American Quarterly* 20 (Fall 1968): 580–95. Most complete account of relationship between the Boss and the Kingfish.

Shepherd, Allen. "Warren's *All the King's Men*: Using the Author's Guide to the Novel." *English Journal* 62 (May 1973): 704–8. Worthwhile comparison of the novel with Warren's own interpretations in essay and interview.

Sillars, Malcolm O. "Warren's *All the King's Men*: A Study in Populism." *American Quarterly* 9 (Fall 1957): 345–53. Examines elements of the American populist movement in the novel.

Slack, Robert C. "The Telemachus Theme." In *"All the King's Men": A Symposium*, 29–38. Pittsburgh, Pa.: Carnegie Press, 1957. The problem of Jack's search for a father as necessary to restore his connections to the world.

Sochatoff, A. Fred. "Some Treatments of the Huey Long Theme." In *"All the King's Men": A Symposium*, 3–15. Pittsburgh, Pa.: Carnegie Press, 1957. The fictional use of Long's career in three modern novels.

Strout, Cushing. *"All the King's Men* and the Shadow of William James." *Southern Review* 6 (Autumn 1970): 920–34. American pragmatism as found in Willie's politics and Jack's morality.

Wilcox, Earl J. "'A Cause for Laughter, A Thing for Tears': Humor in *All the King's Men*." *Southern Literary Journal* 12 (Fall 1979): 27–35. Changes in Jack's humor related to his spiritual growth.

Index

Adams, Henry: *Democracy*, 10
All the King's Men: criticism of, 15-
    18; drama version, 6-7;
    importance of, 11; issues in,
    21, 112; moral corruption in,
    64; movie version, 12-13; nar-
    rative form of, 25-30, 48; as a
    political novel, 9-10; publica-
    tion of, 12; reviews of, 13-15;
    road trip as motif, 31-33, 52-
    53, 82-83, 104, 113; setting
    of, 22; significance of names
    in, 23-24; as top ten work, 18;
    universal conflict in, 22, 109;
    Warren's essay on, 17

Basso, Hamilton: *Sun in Capricorn*,
    10, 13
Black population, 35
Bradbury, John M., 16
Brontë, Charlotte, 51
Burden, Jack: attitude of, 111; at
    Burden's Landing, 48-51; con-
flict with Old South, 46-47,
84, 96; and Ellis Burden, 65-
67; as follower of Stark, 56,
73, 91; as graduate student,
45, 55-58, 61-63, 87; Great
Sleeps, 45-46, 49, 83, 88, 105;
Great Twitch philosophy, 90,
111; and the hospital, 80;
investigation of Governor
Stanton, 76-78; investigation
of Judge Irwin, 38, 63, 65, 70,
72, 93, 97; lack of ambition,
57-58, 85, 87; in love with
Anne Stanton, 37, 50, 59, 80,
81, 82, 83-88, 107; and the
Mastern journals, 55-56, 58,
61-63, 108, 110; as narrator,
11, 26-30, 39, 47, 53-54, 65,
81-83, 88, 96, 99, 103, 113;
real father, 58, 89, 94, 103,
112; rebirth of, 106-107, 110,
112, 113; as reporter, 34, 40,
43; significance of name, 23;

as Stark's research assistant, 35, 65, 105, 110; stepfathers of, 50; subplot chronology, 28-29

Burden's Landing, 37, 48-49, 51, 84, 93, 104

Cargill, Oscar, 15
Civil War, 61, 68, 77
Conrad, Joseph: *Nostromo*, 9
Crawford, Broderick, 13

Davis, Robert, 14
Deep South, 22
Dos Passos, John: *The Grand Design*, 10; *Number One*, 10
Dostoyevski, Fyodor: *The Possessed*, 9
Drury, Allen: *Advise and Consent*, 10

Faulkner, William. *See* Southern Literary Renaissance
Frohock, W. M., 15

Gardiner, Harold, 13
Garland, Hamlin: *A Spoil of Office*, 10
Girault, Norton R., 15
Good old boys, 39-41, 53

Hawthorne, Nathaniel: *The Scarlet Letter*, 23
Heilman, Robert B., 15
Hicks, Granville, 14
Hitler, Adolf, 3
Huey's Cossacks, 6

Irwin, Montague, Judge: home of, 37, 51; investigation of, 65; and Mabel Carruthers, 71; meetings with Stark and Burden, 37-38; as Stark's antagonist, 36; as substitute father, 49; suicide of, 92-94, 103

James, Henry: *The American*, 23

Katope, Christopher G., 16
Kerr, Elizabeth, 16
Koestler, Arthur: *Darkness at Noon*, 9

Langely, Adria Locke: *A Lion Is in the Streets*, 10
London, Jack: *The Iron Heel*, 10
Long, Huey: accomplishments (1928-35), 6; assassination of, 7; assistance to lower classes, 5,6; association with LSU, 4; as basis for Willie Stark, 7; as governor, 4; as "Kingfish," 7; and the "Long Revolution," 5; as senator, 4; other works about, 10
Long Revolution, 5
Longism, 5
Louisiana, 3-6, 32, 82

Machiavelli: *The Prince*, 3
Mason City, 31-34, 40, 45
Mastern, Cass: death of, 61; diary of, 27; journals and letters, 55; story of, 56, 58-61, 67, 86; subplot chronology, 28
Mayberry, George, 14
McCambridge, Mercedes, 13
Meckier, Jerome, 16
Minor characters in *All the King's Men*
  Burden, Ellis, 51, 66-67, 83, 94, 108, 112; Burden, Mrs., 49-51, 57-58, 93, 94-95, 107; Burke, Sadie, 36, 43-44, 51, 53, 63, 70, 101, 104; Coffee,

Hubert, 91; Duffy, Tiny, 32, 35, 43, 70, 76, 99, 101, 104, 105; Frey, Sibyl, 92, 97, 98, 106; Larson, Gummy, 70, 91, 97-98; Littlepaugh, Lili Mae, 72, 77; Littlepaugh, Mortimer, 72, 94; MacMurfee, 42, 45, 92-93, 97; Miller, Hugh 52, 108; O'Sheehan, Sugar Boy, 32-33, 52, 105; Phebe, 60-61; Seager, Lois, 82, 87; Stanton, Adam, 37, 46, 50, 66, 68-70, 76, 78, 81, 90, 98; 100-101, 105; Stanton, Anne, 37, 44, 46, 50, 66, 68-71, 77-78, 80-81, 83-88, 91, 99, 100, 104; Stanton, Governor, 64, 68, 71, 76, 77, 101; Stark, Lucy, 32, 34, 36, 41, 52-53, 68, 75, 102, 106–7; Stark, Tom, 32, 67-68, 74,75, 81, 92, 97, 98-99, 106; Trice, Annabelle, 44, 59-60, 62-63; Trice, Duncan, 59-60, 62-63; White, Byram, 51-52

Mussolini, Benito, 3

Nakadate, Neil, 16
New South, 22-23, 31, 34, 37-38, 49, 57, 69, 78, 92, 108, 113

O'Connor, Edwin: *The Last Hurrah*, 10
Old South, 22, 31, 35, 37-38, 40, 46-48, 52, 58-59, 68-69, 71, 76, 77, 78, 83, 89, 92, 101, 108, 113

Payne, Ladell, 15
Poe, Edgar Allan, 50
Porter, Katherine Anne. *See* Southern Literary Renaissance
Prescott, Orville, 13, 15

Rago, Henry, 14
Rossen, Robert, 12
Shakespeare, William: *Julius Caesar*, 3
Sinclair, Upton: *Oil!*, 10
Southern belle, 37, 50, 58-60, 69, 81, 84, 86, 100
Southern Literary Renaissance, 21-22, 32; Faulkner, 21; Porter, 22; Tate, 21-22; Wolfe, 22
Stark, Willie: adulterous affairs of, 63, 81, 91, 100; appearance of, 35; assassination of, 99-102; birthplace of, 32; campaign for governor, 42-45; campaigns for county treasurer, 39-42; as demagogue, 53, 76, 102, 110; hospital, 52, 74, 75, 80; impeachment of, 52-54; married life of, 36; paradox of, 54; parallels to Huey Long, 7; philosophy of good and evil, 78-80; political career of, 33-35, 97, 109; reformation of, 99, 102; role in White's impeachment, 51-52; school board scandal, 40-42; significance of name, 23; and son Tom, 67-68, 75, 92, 98-99, 102; subplot chronology, 29
Standard Oil Company, 5
State Bureau of Identification, The - see Huey's Cossacks
Stowe, Harriet Beecher: *Uncle Tom's Cabin*, 10

Tate, Allen. *See* Southern Literary Renaissance
Trilling, Diana, 14
Trilling, Lionel: *The Middle of the Journey*, 10
Tate, Allen. *See* Southern Literary Renaissance

Warren, Robert Penn: dictators and politics, 4; drama version of *All the King's Men*, 6-7; Guggenheim Fellowship, 3; in Italy, 3; at LSU 3, 4; writing through Jack Burden, 45

Weiss, Carl, Dr., 7
Wolfe, Thomas. *See* Southern Literary Renaissance
Wood, J. P., 14

The Author

Harold Woodell teaches southern literature in the English department at Clemson University. The author of several articles on southern fiction, he is the editor of *The Shattered Dream: A Southern Bride at the Turn of the Century* (1990), a diary written by a southern belle. He also edits the annual *Proceedings of the Thomas Wolfe Society*.

(continued from the front flap)

THE AUTHOR

Harold Woodell, who teaches southern literature at Clemson University, is the editor of *The Shattered Dream: A Southern Bride at the Turn of the Century* and *The Proceedings of the Thomas Wolfe Society*, as well as a frequent writer of articles on southern fiction.

RELATED AND RECENT TITLES AVAILABLE IN TWAYNE'S MASTERWORK STUDIES SERIES

The Awakening by Joyce Dyer
Babbitt by Glen Love
The Catcher in the Rye by Sanford Pinsker
The Crucible by James J. Martine
The Death of Ivan Ilich by Gary Jahn
Frankenstein by Mary Lowe-Evans
Lord of the Flies by Patrick Reilly
Oedipus Tyrannus by Charles Segal
Oliver Twist by Richard Dunn
A Passage to India by Judith Scherer Herz
Le Père Goriot by Martin Kanes
The Plague by Steven Kellman
Saint Joan by Arnold Silver
The Trial by Henry Sussman
Troilus and Criseyde by Allen Frantzen
Washington Square by Ian F. A. Bell

TWAYNE PUBLISHERS
An Imprint of Macmillan Publishing Company
866 Third Avenue
New York, New York 10022
© 1993 Twayne Publishers